# MARTYRED AT FIRST SIGHT:

## THE REALITY OF REALITY TV

BY RICHELLE AMINA

# DISCLAIMER

This book is a work of nonfiction based on my personal experience as a participant on a UK reality television show. All events are recounted to the best of my memory and reflect my honest impressions, emotional truth, and the impact those experiences had on my life.

To protect the privacy of individuals involved, some names, physical details, and identifying characteristics have been changed or withheld. In cases where dialogue or events are described, they are based on recollections of real interactions and, where necessary, have been paraphrased, condensed, or dramatised for clarity and narrative flow.

While I have made every effort to be truthful and accurate, this is not a transcript - it is my lived experience. Any opinions expressed are mine alone and do not reflect those of any broadcaster, production company, or affiliated parties.

This book addresses matters that I believe are in the public interest, including issues of welfare, consent, and the ethical treatment of reality TV participants. It is not written to harm or defame, but to expose harmful practices, challenge damaging narratives, and to give voice to what has too often been silenced.



For permissions or inquiries, contact: Skuntpublishing@gmail.com

First published in June 2025

Print ISBN: 978-1-0369-2211-5

Ebook ISBN: 978-1-0369-2212-2

Printed in the United Kingdom by Amina Publishing

This book was written by the author, with the support of AI as a creative tool.

Edited by Kim Graves

Cover Design by Richelle Amina

Interior Layout Design by Mila Popovic

# DEDICATION

For my daughter, who I'd burn it all down for.

Love, Mum

# PREFACE:
# A MATTER OF PUBLIC INTEREST

This book has been written in the public interest.

It documents personal experiences that intersect with systemic failures in the reality television industry, failures that carry serious implications for health, safety, and ethical standards. The events described are based on my direct participation in a widely broadcast programme, and every reasonable effort has been made to ensure accuracy and fairness.

The contents expose practices that go far beyond one individual's story. These include the concealment of medical information, the manipulation of consent, and the psychological and reputational damage that can result from deliberate editorial distortion. They also include the unequal treatment of women in both production and public reception.

Publishing this material is not an act of retaliation. It is an act of accountability. Where individuals and organisations wield power behind closed doors, there must be space for scrutiny, transparency, and informed discussion. That is the intention of this work.

The public has a right to know how these systems operate- and who they protect.

# ACKNOWLEDGEMENTS

To my friends: you didn't sign up for this, but you took every blow like it was nothing - and kept it moving.

**Amanda**, You were there from the first crack to the complete collapse - watching it all unravel while standing solid beside me. Protective when I didn't know I needed protecting. Angry on my behalf when I was too numb to feel it. And still, somehow, remained luminous in the wreckage.

**Dee,** You didn't just clap back. You went full scorched earth. The precision. The rage. The elegance of your violence. They never stood a chance. I've never been prouder to watch someone ruin lives in my defence. And to the woman who messaged me in tears over Dee -when I said I didn't know who you were talking about, I lied. I knew exactly who you meant. And honestly? Serves you right.

**David**, I admire your commitment to believing men were decent. I hated being the one to shatter the illusion. But I'm glad you're coming around to the realisation. Thank you for sitting through the tears. It takes a village to raise a single woman, and you've been one hell of a village.

**Sharon,** I looked you dead in the eye and swore I'd done nothing wrong. Then the episodes dropped, and you were left defending my honour like a barrister with no brief. And still - you never flinched. Thanks for trying to convince your colleagues I was normal. It was bold of you.

**Uriah**, To my big brother and forever protector, thank you for walking me down that aisle like it was a mission, not a moment. You didn't just show up you locked in, held it down, and made sure I was laughing (and absolutely steaming drunk) when I needed it most. You even brushed off your friends when they asked, "What the hell is wrong with your friend?" You were my wedding ride or die. I wouldn't have done any of it without you.

**Janey**, you trusted the 'science', beamed like a proud mum at the wedding, then when the shit hit the fan, you roared like a lioness and reminded them exactly who you are.

**My daughter**, Now 22 years old. My anchor in the chaos. Days before the wedding, when I was unravelling and totally prepared to disappear into the Thames, you didn't panic. You calmly suggested we Google how to fake my death. Not as a joke but as a viable escape route. You saw me spiralling and didn't flinch. You just opened a new tab and started plotting. It was unhinged and hilarious, I love that you inherited my dark little sense of humour. Through all the madness, you never stopped being proud of your mum, and every day you remind me: yep, she's definitely mine.

*And*

To the women I shared the screen with - this book is for you too. You were brilliant, messy, sharp, vulnerable, and so much more than what was shown. You held your ground in a system designed to strip us down to types: I saw your strength in real-time. I saw how much it cost you.

We were thrown into something we didn't fully understand but we survived it. Now I get to write the version in which we're not just plot points in someone else's drama.

This one's for us.

# CONTENTS

# INTRODUCTION

## THIS WAS NEVER JUST A TV SHOW

I didn't walk into reality TV thinking it would ruin my life. That's not the kind of thing you expect when you're promised compatibility, science, and a team of "experts" with clipboards and kind eyes. Like most people, I thought Martyred at First Sight UK (as I now call it) was extreme - but exciting. What could be more romantic (and slightly unhinged) than marrying a complete stranger in front of the nation?

## SPOILER: A LOT OF THINGS

I didn't apply because I was in a desperate situation. I wasn't clinging to a last hope. I was curious - intrigued by the idea that maybe, just maybe, science could do better than my track record. I'd done dating apps, introductions, even sitting in cafés trying to look (un)approachable. So, when a TV show offered matchmaking by experts, I thought, Why not? Let them do the emotional admin for once.

There was a part of me - the idealistic part, the rom-com-raised part - that genuinely believed they might find someone who matched my energy, my values, my life. I wasn't asking for a fairy tale. Just someone honest, interesting, kind. Someone who didn't lie. Someone who didn't come with a medical hazard taped to their trousers.

Instead, I got a storyline.

I was 48, one of the oldest women to appear on the series and I wanted to represent something rarely seen on reality TV: a grown woman with experience, self-respect, and no interest in playing dumb for airtime.

I went in thinking reality TV was finally making space for women like me. Turns out, they weren't opening a door - they were laying a trap. I thought I was stepping into an experiment about love and relationships. What I got was something far more calculated, far more damaging, and far less "real" than I could've imagined. The real twist wasn't the matchmaking - it was the betrayal of trust by the show, the production company, and an industry that sells exploitation as entertainment.

This book isn't about heartbreak. It's about betrayal. About what happens when ethics are optional, when women are served up for spectacle, and when producers control the story while pretending they're capturing truth. It's about being cast as a character in a script you never got to read - and then being hated for it.

And it's about what came after - the abuse, the headlines, the strangers who thought they knew me because of a 45-minute edit. People who posted about my employer, my face, my voice - like I wasn't real either.

But I am real. And this is my experience. I've held the screenshots. I've sat with the trauma. I've found the humour in the madness. And I've spoken to others who've been through it too.

This is my first book - and no producers were harmed (unfortunately) in the making of it.

# CHAPTER 1:

## MATCH MADE FOR RATINGS

## THE COLD FRONT

The first commitment ceremony was set in what I can only describe as a meat locker with curtains. That room was *freezing*. I don't mean chilly - I mean teeth-chattering, toe-numbing, "should I be seeing my own breath indoors?" kind of cold. We were huddled in rows of cold, hard chairs like kids in detention at an Arctic boot camp. Every time someone sighed, you could see condensation drifting into the air like we were vaping our misery.

We sat there for hours. Literally hours. No blankets. No heaters. It was as if the temperature had been deliberately set to strip us of all warmth - physically and emotionally. By the time the experts emerged to deliver their lines, I half-expected them to skate in wearing fur capes.

As we entered the meat locker for every commitment ceremony, the experts would stand there deadly silent, lined up like soldiers on parade - backs straight, arms clasped, expressions solemn. As if their sheer posture alone could inject some kind of authority into the circus. It was all part of the theatre, of course. Make the room cold, make the cast uncomfortable and intimidated, and plant three experts like judges in a dystopian school assembly - instant tension. Melinda with her headmistress glare, Charmagne barely whispering like a haunted librarian, and P-Dawg looking like he was about to hand down a prison sentence. It was laughable. Manufactured gravitas. All this pomp and poise, just to ask whether we'd like to stay married to the stranger who ruined our week.

## HUMAN CENTRAL HEATING

My toes had fully frozen inside my boots. I kept wiggling them just to check they were still attached. At one point, I looked at Orton - this man I was supposed to be married to - and without a word, we huddled together like penguins in a David Attenborough documentary. Not out of love. Not out of chemistry. Just out of sheer survival instinct. Human central heating. It was the only time we had anything resembling genuine intimacy - a joint effort to avoid hypothermia before being paraded in front of the "experts."

And still, no one blinked. Not a single producer thought, *maybe these people shouldn't be one sniffle away from pneumonia.* We were props in a cold box, warming each other like two strangers on a delayed train.

## COMMITMENT CEREMONY OR CHAOS REVUE?

It was like a scene out of a Mike Leigh satire meets a weather emergency broadcast. We were frozen solid, blowing clouds of condensation into the air, shivering in our boots like Victorian orphans waiting for gruel. Somewhere between our third hour of emotional frostbite, Emma leaned over to me - eyes wide, voice hushed in that Etonian tone only Barnes'y gets away with - and whispered, *"He doesn't fancy me."* Like it was the final plot twist in a murder mystery and not just a polite shrug of romantic disinterest.

Meanwhile, Caspar was in the corner muttering "for fuck's sake" on a loop like a malfunctioning Alexa. Lacey looked like she was about to pass out - and then she did. Full-on fainted. And P-Dawg Brut, bless his polished bald head, managed to make Sacha cry - not from insight, not from revelation, but just from whatever self-help monologue he had rehearsed that day.

It was total chaos. Emotional triage in a walk-in freezer. And yet, no one stopped. No one said, "Shall we pause this and check everyone's vitals?" Because in reality TV, a woman fainting is just a cutaway. A man swearing is character development. And a cast member sobbing on camera? That's BAFTA bait.

And P-Dawg Brut - who, to be clear, is not bald, just slick - turned on Sacha like she'd just insulted his mother, snapping at her for shouting out during the ceremony. What made it surreal was that five minutes earlier, a producer had walked right over to us, shivering crew, and all, and *told us* to speak up more. To "give them something." So, Sacha did exactly that - followed the cue, brought the energy - and suddenly she was getting disciplined like a child in assembly.

He turned it into a lesson about respect and timing, completely ignoring the fact that we were in a pressure cooker wrapped in a walk-in freezer, being puppeteered like pantomime characters. Sacha was humiliated.

You could see her face drop - not just from embarrassment, but from that dawning realisation we were all having: *we are not people in this room; we are props with microphones.*

## THE "EXPERTS" IN LAB COATS

They loved to remind us that this was a "scientific experiment." The word *science* got thrown around so much I half expected someone to walk in with a microscope. It was the branding - the illusion of logic and data, all neatly wrapped in jargon. But behind the clipboards and buzzwords was something messier. They weren't matchmaking; they were casting.

And of course, there was Melinda. Sitting there like the school headmistress who's just caught two kids fighting over a Bunsen burner. Not saying much, just frowning, tilting her head, and nodding along like her neck was on a spring. The expert equivalent of a bobblehead. You know the type - the quiet one who doesn't say much, but when she does, it's always something like, *"You both need to respect the process,"* even when one of you has just been hit with a truth bomb and the other one's been lying through his teeth for weeks.

And then there was P-Dawg. Sitting there like the oracle of love, arms folded, eyes narrowing into faux empathy. Thankfully, by this point, he'd retired those awful leather Jesus sandals he used to wear - and truly, hallelujah for that small mercy. I spent half the early shows wondering if he was going to bless someone with olive oil or just whip out a tambourine. But now, sandal-free, and deadly serious, he too had nothing to offer. Just the occasional knowing nod, like he was watching a performance only he understood. But when it came to actual answers - about why they'd matched me with a man who could barely tell the truth - he had nothing. Zip. It was all philosophy and smooth soundbites until the moment demanded actual accountability. Then suddenly he was a monk on mute.

And then there was Charmagne. The one who barely spoke. I used to wonder if her mic was even switched on. But no - it was. She was just terrified to use it. It wasn't just when the cameras were rolling, either. Even off-mic, off-camera, when we were supposedly "safe," she kept her voice low like MI5 were monitoring her through the Ficus. I always got the sense she had a heart in there somewhere - maybe even a conscience - but she also had a mortgage. And in this industry, survival often means saying nothing while watching everything. You could practically see the conflict in her eyes: *this is wrong, but I need the work.* And so, she'd nod and smile and avoid eye contact, like a guest at a dinner party where someone's about to be stabbed with a steak knife but no one wants to ruin the dessert.

It was like being gaslit by the cast of *Inside Out,* but they only had two emotions between them: smug and silent. Melinda's job, it seemed, was to project authority without offering anything concrete. She was there to keep us in line - the disciplinarian in a feather blouse - while nodding at absolute nonsense as if it were sacred scripture.

The moment I truly began to see through the façade was when they stopped responding like professionals and started sounding like PR reps. No real concern, no solutions - just the gentle hum of damage control.

The irony? I trusted the experts more than I trusted the production team. Until I realised, they were one and the same.

## THE SILENT TREATMENT

We asked them straight. Sat on the couch, both of us looking at these so-called "experts" and asked: *Why did you match us?* And you'd think we'd asked them to explain quantum physics using sock puppets. All three just sat there, blinking like they were buffering. Not one word. Not even a fake answer. The silence was deafening - and hilarious if you weren't living it.

Because up until then, they'd never shut up. "We matched you based on values." "We saw your potential as a couple." "We used science, psychology, compatibility metrics..." Honestly, they made it sound like they'd cracked the human heart like a maths equation. But now? When asked for one shred of logic behind this tragic pairing? Nada. It was like someone had unplugged their programming.

And I realised: they weren't scientists. They were storytellers in lab coats, selling fairy dust in clipboards. And in that moment, even my "husband" looked stunned. Which really says something.

## SCIENCE, SHENANIGANS AND STDS

I said yes to the experiment because I was open to love and compatibility. Not open to being lied to. Not open to being matched with someone wildly incompatible - and definitely not open to being paired with someone who had a medical issue and never disclosed it to me. You'd think that would be the bare minimum: basic honesty and not putting someone's health at risk. But in reality TV, drama is the only currency. And a woman feeling "uncomfortable" doesn't trend on Twitter - but a woman "overreacting" does.

From the very beginning, something felt off. The chemistry? Non-existent. The conversation? Evasive. I was asking too many questions at the "wedding", god forbid. Painfully strained. The 'process' felt less like a match and more like a blind date in a dystopian simulation. But I smiled. I laughed politely. I played along. Because by then, smiling through the awkwardness had become my full-time job.

The producers had insisted he was my perfect fit. "Trust the process," they said, parroting the show's favourite line like it was gospel. But the process seemed to involve ignoring every red flag and manufacturing tension like it was part of the wedding catering. And because I didn't fall head over heels for him in the first hour of filming, I was instantly recast as cold. Difficult. Dismissive. You could practically hear the villain soundtrack cue up behind me.

What they didn't show was the effort I was making - the way I tried to stay open, to stay hopeful, even when I knew deep down this was wrong. They didn't show the kindness, the confusion, the doubt. They just showed what fit the script. It didn't matter what I said, how I acted, or how many times I tried to explain myself - the edit was locked in. The production team weren't filming to understand me; they were filming to confirm a narrative they'd already written for editing. I could've given the Dalai Lama a piggyback ride and they'd still cut it to look like I'd run him over. Once they'd boxed me as "the difficult one," every moment was framed to serve that story. And I started to feel it - the quiet shift in how my scenes were being steered, how questions were intended to lead me straight into landmines.

But off-camera, things got worse. Much worse.

My "husband" wasn't just emotionally incompatible. He was evasive, inconsistent, and as I would come to learn, hiding something serious. Something that, had I known from the start, would have changed everything. The producers knew. They had organised the medical testing for all cast. And when I raised the issue upon my exit from this horror show, they told me something to the effect of *"It was only low- level. If we didn't cast people with STDs, we wouldn't have a cast."*

I remember blinking at the sentence, trying to process it. As if it were obvious. As if that logic - that collective lie - somehow made it acceptable.

They had offered me no warning. No conversation. No offer of protection or concern for my well-being. Just shrugs. A carefully rehearsed distance. And that's when the penny dropped: this wasn't about love. It wasn't even about science. It was about *content*. Drama. Clicks. And a woman feeling violated doesn't trend - but a woman who's angry and loud? That's TV gold.

That line - "If we didn't cast people with STDs, we wouldn't have a cast" - stuck with me. Not just for the casual cruelty of it, but for what it revealed. The tests weren't about safety. They were about liability. A tick-box exercise so the showmakers could claim they'd "done their part."

And really - why make us go through medical testing at all if you'll ignore the results? Why pretend it's a safe, scientific match when you're knowingly putting people in harm's way?

During the 'honeymoon' Orton told me one of the executive producers approached him gushing after our match and said proudly, "Didn't we do well?" He told me innocently. Naively however all I could think was no one said that to me. It felt like I'd been handed to him on a platter. A gift. A pawn. A plot device in someone else's storyline.

That's the trick of it. You come in with confidence, with boundaries, and by the second week, you're apologising for having instincts. You start doubting your gut because everyone around you is pretending this is normal.

What wasn't normal was the way they edited me. The way I watched whole parts of myself - my humour, warmth, humanity - sliced out like a bad take. In their version, I was standoffish. Cold. One-dimensional. They shaped the footage like Play-Doh, squeezing it into a storyline that didn't match reality but looked great at 9 p.m. on a Wednesday night.

And when it aired? That's when the real damage began.

I trended. Not for being brave. Not for being honest. Not for walking away.

I trended for being a "stuck-up bitch."

The public labelled me vile. Abusive. Mentally unstable. They didn't know me, of course - but that didn't matter. They'd seen the version of me the show wanted them to see: eyerolls with no context, silences framed as disdain, reactions to conversations that had been edited out entirely.

My DMs turned into a war zone. The messages came in fast and unrelenting. "That's why you're single bitch." "You're everything wrong with modern women." "You should die." "Apologise to him on live TV."

It wasn't just viewers. It was gossip accounts. YouTube commentators. Tik Tok "body language experts." People who swore they could diagnose personality disorders from a 15-second clip.

There was an ecosystem of hate, and I was the trending topic of the week.

But this wasn't just a bad date caught on camera. This was a system - one that chews women up, edits them into villains, and calls it entertainment. A machine built on selective empathy and manufactured storylines.

I came in expecting safety as a bare minimum and walked out with a warning.

Because what happened to me wasn't an accident. It was by design. And once you see the machine behind the curtain, you can't unsee it.

You just have to decide whether you're going to stay silent - or name it.

And I've chosen to name it.[1]

1 Disclaimer: The events and experiences described in this chapter reflect the author's personal recollection and perspective. Some dialogue has been paraphrased, condensed, or altered for clarity. Names and identifying details have been changed or withheld to protect privacy. Interpretations of motives and behaviour are the author's own and based on how they were experienced at the time.

# CHAPTER 2:
# MADE FOR HIS STORYLINE

## ACTING SCHOOL DROPOUT ENERGY

Filming with "my husband" was like working opposite someone auditioning for a low-budget web series no one asked for. The minute the cameras rolled he slipped into character. Not over-the-top - just calculated. He wasn't reacting, he was performing. Doing exactly what he thought they wanted. Saying the lines, hitting the beats. Badly.

Off camera? He was passive, weirdly smug, and obsessed with his image while maintaining a docile persona. Overall, he was harmless. Harmless, in the way poison is harmless once you've developed the antidote. I built mine from every disappointment he reminds me of.

On camera? He was every man who's ever practiced speeches in the mirror and thinks that makes him emotionally intelligent.

I wasn't talking to a person. I was talking to a performance - and not a particularly strong one.

## ARRIVAL: GLAMOUR? NOT QUITE.

When we landed in Mauritius, we weren't glowing honeymooners stepping into paradise. We were exhausted, greasy, and practically feral. The production company, ever the picture of luxury, had booked the most convoluted route imaginable. By the time we arrived, I felt like I'd backpacked there on foot. We were unwashed, sleep-deprived, and dragging our cases like broken contestants on *The Amazing Race: Emotionally Unprepared Edition.*

It was obvious they were making this on a shoestring. The budget was so low I'm honestly surprised they didn't hand me the camera and ask me to film my own breakdown. The five of us turned up at the hotel hauling suitcases and camera gear like overworked interns on a student film. No welcome, no magic - just us, sweating through our own production like unpaid extras in the love story we were meant to be starring in.

Orton was already struggling. Physically, emotionally, and spiritually- you name it. Despite everything I'd already begun to sense, I supported him. I supported *us.* I was conscious of the cameras, but more conscious that this was just the beginning of what would be a gruelling, performative schedule, strung together by long shoots, fake moments, and forced intimacy.

In that moment, I showed up. Not for the show, not for the audience, but for a man I'd just fake married on paper, because I still had hope that maybe, just maybe, something real could come from all this madness.

## TRAPPED ABROAD WITH A WALKING RED FLAG

We were on the second or third night of the honeymoon when Orton suddenly announced he "had the feels". Of course, he waited until the cameras were rolling to do it. Not a second before. No warning, no quiet chat, no "hey, just so you're not blindsided"-just vibes and a full film crew. You'd think if someone genuinely had feelings for you, they might want to see your actual reaction first, not hand it straight over to production like a press release. But no. This was his moment. And when I didn't immediately melt into a grateful puddle of tears and fairy lights, the producer got *angry* at me.

I'd ruined their perfectly good scene of manufactured romance. Sorry I didn't follow the script I wasn't given. My job was to play the doting wife to a man I didn't trust, after five days of awkward silences and him trying to emotionally speed run intimacy for airtime. He was there pitching a love story, and I was still trying to figure out if we even liked the same temperature on the aircon. But heaven forbid I take a second to react like a real person. The producer practically hissed, "You need to give us *something*." My confusion wasn't usable content. Sorry for not collapsing into your carefully edited narrative, babe.

## NIGHTLY BROADCAST: THE CHEATING CHRONICLES

Every evening at dinner, without fail, he'd deliver the same tragic monologue about being cheated on as if it were a bedtime story he'd memorised, rehearsed, and now felt compelled to perform nightly for the nation. Same tone, same pacing, same sighs for dramatic effect. I started to feel like I was trapped in a low-budget reboot of *Love Actually*, except all the cue cards just said, "She Cheated."

There was no variation. No reflection. Just rinse and repeat heartbreak, projected onto me as if I'd personally crawled through the vents to betray him myself. At first I tried to empathise, genuinely. But by day four, I was emotionally held hostage by someone else's trauma, reliving a relationship I had never been part of.

Food was my coping mechanism. I ate. Like a pig. No shame, no restraint. It was the only thing that got me through. Every bite was a small act of rebellion. I had plates in front of me - his and mine. Starters, mains, sides, double desserts. If I was going to be dragged through a fake honeymoon with a man clinging to decade-old rejection like it was a personality trait, then I was going to eat like I'd earned it. Cutlery in both hands, chewing through, a woman on a mission. If they were going to call me the villain, I'd at least be a well-fed one.

Even the producers looked like they'd aged five years. Sweating through their tropical linen, clinging to their cameras with sweaty palms but still nodding encouragingly, knowing they had to "get that scene." This wasn't just a moment; it was content. It didn't matter how tired we all were - emotionally, physically, spiritually - as long as he got to deliver his nightly soliloquy like a man auditioning for sympathy instead of connection.

## NOT A MORNING PERSON, NOT EVEN CLOSE

Don't even get me started on the mornings. I've never been a morning person. Never claimed to be. Mornings, to me, are something to be endured, not celebrated.

Before I peel myself off the mattress, I'm just a haunted shell with direct debits. So, waking up in a luxury hotel in Mauritius with cameras waiting outside my bedroom door wasn't just jarring - it was violent.

They'd send junior producers to knock. Softly at first, then with the desperation of someone who knew the filming schedule was tighter than my patience. Some days I'd hear the whispering before I opened my eyes. Other days, I'd wake up mid-sentence because one of them had crept in like it was a hostage negotiation.

Apparently, being semi-conscious was no excuse. There was content to film and a narrative to build. Me not wanting to discuss the state of my fake marriage before 8 a.m.? "Uncooperative."

Imagine being woken up to talk about someone else's heartbreak you didn't cause, on camera, before you've even had a cup of tea. Welcome to reality TV.

I wasn't expecting a luxury escape, but I also wasn't expecting to be yanked out of bed at sunrise by twitchy, sleep-deprived "welfare" producers who treated personal space like a suggestion and boundaries like an inconvenience.

But one morning stands out more than the rest. I'd just had a nightmare - a vivid, disorienting mess where I was trapped in a marriage I didn't want, tethered to a man I didn't choose. I jolted awake, panicked, and disoriented... only to find Orton's actual face hovering inches from mine.

"Babe, time to get up. They're ready to film."

It wasn't a nightmare. It was real.

I lay there for a second, genuinely wondering if I was still dreaming or if I'd accidentally joined some kind of social experiment where punishment looked like a honeymoon. No time to process, though. The junior producers were already whispering by the room door, ready to capture my reaction to another day of emotional gymnastics I hadn't trained for.

It seemed that needing five minutes to emotionally stabilise before being filmed wasn't part of the contract.

## POSTCARD VIEWS, PICNIC FROM HELL

The Seven Valleys in Mauritius were breath-taking - lush, green, cinematic. The kind of place you'd expect to have a spiritual awakening or at least a peaceful moment. Instead, I was sat on a damp blanket, in the rain, pretending to eat wet sandwiches. You know it's bad when even the cling film looks like it's given up.

The producers called it a "romantic picnic." I called it public humiliation with snacks. Locals and tourists on actual holidays hiked past us looking baffled, as if we were some kind of unhinged honeymoon art piece: two miserable people on wet rocks, flanked by a camera crew, pretending this was romantic.

I wanted to melt into the moss. The cameras were rolling, the sky was crying, and he was once again mid-monologue about his ex. I thought, "Is this my villain origin story?" Because there's nothing quite like trying to look emotionally open while your food disintegrates, and strangers watch you feign enjoyment.

## JULIA'S STONE

That same night on the honeymoon, I actually started to feel like myself again. I'd met a couple at the resort - normal, funny, and kind. The sort of people on an actual holiday, not trapped in a fake marriage with a camera crew orbiting their misery. Orton was in the hotel room, and for the first time all week, I felt relaxed. We drank, laughed, swapped stories, and I remember thinking, *this is what this trip could've been.* Then, like a bad plot twist, I saw a shadow moving through the darkness. Orton. Coming to look for his "wife."

Just like that, the moment was gone. The spell broke, the laughter shrank, and I left with him. Back to the room. Back to the role.

I called it a night like a dutiful wife, and before I left Julia, my new honeymoon bestie, gave me a small stone, something she picked up from the beach. I told her I'd put it on the microwave when I got back to the apartment, and I did. A small nod to something real in a week full of performance. When the show aired, she messaged me: *I saw the stone.* That meant more than I expected. Proof that someone, even briefly, saw me.

All of it - the rain-soaked picnics, the nightly sob stories, the emotional ambushes - blended into one long, surreal performance I had never agreed to star in. I was surviving, not thriving. And while the cameras captured the chaos, they missed the exhaustion. The erosion. The quiet parts that explain everything.

## CAMERA-READY INTEGRITY

Having said all that, we *did* have some fun moments. Little pockets of calm where we actually laughed or just enjoyed each other's company without a camera shoved in our faces or a producer fishing for tears. They were rare, but they were real. Not enough to build anything lasting but enough to remind me that it wasn't all doom and trauma dumps.

Of course, none of that made the cut. Because what's a bit of warmth when they can show you rolling your eyes in slow motion instead?

One night however, we were both wrecked. Sweaty, irritable, drained. I was also full, obviously, because eating was the only part of the day I had control over. We'd just finished some chaotic Latin dancing segment that we'd enjoyed, and during what they loosely called a "break," when he snapped. He said we weren't going back upstairs to film. He was certain, calm, and commanding, like he finally meant what he was saying. For a second, I let myself feel relief. Maybe he'd finally decided to draw a line. Maybe, just once, I wouldn't have to be the difficult one.

For that second, I thought he was showing some leadership. But as soon as the producer walked over, that spine vanished. "She doesn't want to film," he said gesturing in my direction, like I'd dragged him out of sync with the schedule. And just like that, I was the problem again. That moment told me everything. He wasn't there to connect - he was there to perform. To look like the consummate professional. Meanwhile, I was just trying to survive the circus without selling off my sanity for screen time. Whatever ease I'd found was shattered the second he threw me under the bus.

Even with the casual bus roll-over, that night we'd enjoyed the Latin dancing as sweaty, chaotic, and ridiculous as it was. The instructor shimmied his hips with the confidence of a man born in sequins, using nothing but rhythm and pelvic persuasion to guide us across the floor. We laughed, we moved, we looked vaguely alive for once. And after all that? It didn't even make the cut. Evidently, joy wasn't on the agenda.

## A PAUSE IN THE PERFORMANCE

In a rare moment of integrity, Orton said no to filming when a producer tried to drag up family issues I have long tried to bury. For that, I thanked him - genuinely. It was one of the only times I felt protected instead of exposed. The producer was pissed.

There were glimmers like that, moments where I thought maybe there was something real to work with. But sadly, hope doesn't survive long under studio lights. Whatever flickers there were, they weren't enough; not against the weight of what we were both being pulled through in that ghastly, grinding process.

## HOME IS WHERE HE TOOK ALL THE HANGERS

There are little moments that tell you everything you need to know about a person. For me, it was the wardrobe. Or rather, the fact that he didn't leave me any space in it. At all. He'd unpacked fully, like we were moving in for six months, not shooting a reality TV farce in a serviced apartment. Every drawer, hanger, and surface were crammed with his clothes, his cologne, his delusion.

I opened the wardrobe expecting a polite half. What I got was a visual monologue that screamed: *This is my space, you're just visiting.* I ended up living out of my suitcase like a guest in my own marriage. Correction: like a hostage in his.

It was so on-brand. This was a man who weaponised monologues and (my)moisturiser with equal intensity. He'd laid claim to the physical space the same way he laid claim to the emotional one - loudly, thoughtlessly, and completely. There was no room for me in the wardrobe, and if I'm honest, there was no room for me in the story either. I was just there to react to it.

If he was chasing a BAFTA, I was chasing the next commitment ceremony. Meat locker or not.

And like any bad screen partner, I ruined the take.

It's not like I was against the whole acting thing. I even asked what kind of roles he was going for - *Top Boy*? A Netflix villain? A walk-on part in *Doctors*? I was genuinely willing to help. But I also started thinking logically: if I had to sit front row for this delusional one-man show, I wanted 10% of his future earnings for five years. Minimum. *Quid pro quo.*

At that point, I stopped engaging from a place of connection and started operating from strategy. What can I get out of this? If I'm going to play along with his shenanigans, his sob stories, his inflated ego, fine. But I want terms. I want compensation. Because let's be honest, I was already doing the emotional labour *and* the scene partner work.

He thought he was giving BAFTA. I was giving an invoice.

## A CAMPAIGN BUILT ON VIBES

Out of nowhere, mid-scene and mid-delusion, he declared he was going to become a politician in St Kitts. Right. Because clearly, the future of Caribbean leadership was going to rise from the ruins of reality TV and the fantasy payroll he kept name-dropping. I asked, more out of morbid curiosity than interest, "What's your political leaning?" He blinked at me, then opened and closed his mouth like a goldfish trying to remember its lines, stared up at the ceiling as if God might beam down the answer, and finally landed on, "Like... Labour?" I wasn't sure if he meant the party or was just paying vague tribute to childbirth.

It was exhausting. Filming with him became a psychological endurance test and made even harder for someone like me, a total novice, because what was I supposed to say?

## DELUSIONS OF GOVERNMENT-BACKED GRANDEUR

The lies weren't just casual, they were cinematic. This wasn't your average exaggeration for a first date. This was *multi-million-pound government contract* territory. Big budget fantasy. He spoke like his LinkedIn was classified, dropping vague references to "government work" like he was moonlighting for MI6, when in reality, he could barely manage a hotel room thermostat.

Every sentence came with a delusion baked in - losing thousands a week by being "on-set", managing payroll (from a Network 4 couch), flipping multiple properties (while running around like an overgrown kid on a school trip), and eyeing a political career (despite not knowing his political leaning)... all somehow balanced around trying to be a reality TV heartthrob.

It was farcical. Delusional. Like watching someone play dress-up in the boardroom of their own imagination. I remember sitting there listening to him ramble while mentally noting that he hadn't left me a single hanger in the wardrobe.

## THE CEO OF NOWHERE

For a man running empires, he hadn't asked for his phone once in a week. When I asked if he ever needed to check his emails, he glared like the concept was beneath him and said, "I have people working for me, you know," like it was perfectly reasonable to juggle multimillion-pound deals from a reality TV set with zero signal and full delusion.

Last I checked, even Bezos, Musk and Dangote have people working for them but still manage to open their inboxes. Or do they?

He wasn't lying to impress me. He was lying to impress the invisible cameras in his mind. This wasn't about love. It was about legacy. In his head, he was already the star of a show that had nothing to do with marriage and everything to do with making himself a myth.

The worst part? I had only asked for a tradesman.

## WRONG SHOW, WRONG CO-STAR

He came on the show to launch an acting career. That much was clear from the moment he told me - on camera - that he'd once been on a billboard in Dubai. I guess in his mind, *Married at First Sight* was less of a social experiment and more of an extended audition reel. Every conversation felt like a scene. Every trauma dump came with a pause for dramatic effect. He wasn't looking for a wife, he was looking for a supporting actress.

Unfortunately for him, I was terrible at the role. I kept missing my cues, forgetting my lines, and worst of all I didn't deliver the emotional validation monologue he clearly expected. I was the kind of co-star who broke character constantly. I asked for logic in the middle of his plotline. I didn't cry when I was supposed to. I didn't gasp when he repeated the same sob story for the fifth night in a row.

## THE TRAGEDY OF THE MATCH

For all the delusion, the contradictions, the emotional monologues, and desperate showmanship he was just a man chasing a dream. And dreams make people do strange things. Uncomfortable things. Sometimes, even unethical things. When you want to be seen badly enough, you'll say what needs to be said, you'll perform, exaggerate, curate, manipulate. Who can blame him? In a world where visibility equals opportunity, this show looked like a shortcut to everything he'd ever wanted: fame, status, perhaps even redemption.

But here's the thing-*I* didn't sign up to be a step on anyone's career ladder. I didn't audition for supporting actress in someone else's comeback story. I was sold the idea of compatibility. Of science-backed connection. What I got was a one-man PR campaign, a walking headline, and a script I never agreed to read from.

Yet, in a strange way, it was just as unfair to him as it was to me. He wasn't looking for a relationship; he was looking for a platform. I wasn't looking for a platform; I was looking for a relationship. So how could this have ever worked? The show paired us like two puzzle pieces from completely different boxes. They knew it would implode. They counted on it. Because implosion makes great TV.

The real tragedy wasn't just that we were mismatched - it's that we were both exploited in different ways. Me, emotionally. Him, aspirationally. And while our motivations couldn't have been more separate, we were both just pawns in someone else's plot.

So no, I don't hate him. I can't. He did what he thought he had to do. But so did I. I tried to stay grounded, to survive the circus, to keep a grip on my dignity while the cameras rolled and the audience sharpened their pitchforks.

The real villain? It wasn't him. And it sure as hell wasn't me.

It was the system that turned our worst match into one of its best storylines.

The truth is, we both endured things. Him in his way, me in mine. We were mismatched, manipulated, and mined for content. The difference was, I saw it for what it was. In the end, neither of us came out clean, but only one of us was ever meant to.

# CHAPTER 3:
# EDIT ME INTO A VILLAIN

## "CAN YOU SAY THAT AGAIN... BUT LIKE A MORON?"

They love to call it "natural," but nothing about filming this show felt remotely real. Producers would stop me mid-sentence and say, *"Can you say that again, but just take out the words ' liar'? Maybe say 'mean' instead?"*

I remember thinking, *You asked me to be honest. Now you want it rewritten in toddler vocabulary.*

They didn't want clarity. They wanted soundbites. Simple. Sharpened. Edited for outrage. If you said something with nuance, they'd ask you to "just simplify it." What they meant was: "Say it in a way that'll get you dragged."

## "NOW JUST STARE OFF INTO THE DISTANCE FOR ME..."

One of the weirdest things about filming a reality show is how often they want you to just... sit. Not talk. Not move. Just sit, staring in contemplation (out of a window preferably) and nod silently. The crew called them ***Noddies*** - shots of you nodding in silence, pretending to listen or react to something that may or may not have happened. Not in the moment, of course.

Then there were the ***GVs*** - general views. Long shots of me walking slowly, looking reflective, up and down the Thames on a windy weekday, - staring pensively out at the water like I was about to throw myself in while tourists and dog walkers weaved past, giving me sideways looks. A producer trotted backwards in front of me with a camera, shouting over the chaos, "Look emotional, but not sad. Now smile! Reflective!" I was reflecting all right - mostly on how ridiculous this all was.

At some point a passer-by eating Doritos gave me a thumbs up, probably thinking it was some student film. I didn't even have the energy to explain.

Those shots you see of someone walking solemnly by the water, deep in thought? Fabricated. Scheduled. Directed. Staged. Usually with a full crew, a portable reflector board, and some poor assistant timing pedestrians. Reality TV? Try public performance art with a mental breakdown storyline.

All of this goes into the ***B-roll*** - the filler footage used to pad out storylines or manipulate the tone of a scene. You know the shots. Someone staring out a window. Looking at their phone. Stirring tea like it's a religious ritual. None of it's spontaneous. It's scheduled. Directed. Sometimes they'll call them *pickups* - extra shots to help "tell the story better" (translation: help the editors Frankenstein something juicy out of scraps).

The result? A narrative stitched together from silent nods and forced pauses. You're not just living it. You're looping it, faking it, performing it in pieces, out of order, for someone else's storyline.

It's easy to laugh at it now - the endless takes, the staged stares, the way they manufactured emotion out of silence. But at the time? It wasn't funny. It was exhausting. I didn't know how any of this worked. I wasn't in on the mechanics or the manipulation. I was just someone doing what I was told, trying to keep up. So, while they were making television, I was genuinely uncomfortable, confused, and being directed like I knew the rules. I didn't. And that's what made it painful.

## VOX POPS FROM HELL

Before and after every single scene - whether you were brushing your teeth or arguing on a balcony - they made us film "**Vox Pops**". Confessionals where you reflect on what *just happened...* even if nothing had.

They'd stop us mid-moment: *"Okay can we just grab you quickly before lunch to do a quick Vox?"*

There is no quicker way to lose your mind than being asked to deliver sincere reactions to events that were either boring, manipulated, or haven't even happened yet. I once had to do a Vox *before* the conversation even took place. Imagine being asked how you feel about a scene you haven't lived through yet. I was reviewing a trailer for a movie I hadn't seen.

They call them "Vox Pops"- short for *Vox populi,* Latin for "voice of the people." Sounds noble, right? Like you're being asked to channel your truth, speak your mind, be raw and real.

What it really means is this: stand - never sit, that would be too comfortable, in front of a camera and feed the beast the lines it needs to stitch a fake story out of your actual life.

We had to film Vox Pops before and after every single scene - whether you were having coffee, going for a walk, arguing, or just blinking at someone too slowly. If a moment was filmed, it had to be framed. And they didn't want your internal monologue. It felt like they wanted you to hit the narrative beats they'd already decided for you.

During early Vox Pops, one of them even tried to coax me into calling myself a cougar - like that's the storyline they wanted to hang me with. As if being a few years older than a man meant I had to lean into some desperate caricature just to give them a soundbite they could twist.

When you'd do one before a conversation even happened.

*"How are you feeling ahead of this chat?"*

I don't know, mate. You tell me - you wrote the script.

The worst part? They'd feed you back your own feelings, just... reworded.

*"So, would you say you were frustrated at that point?"*

Not really.

*"Okay but maybe just say you were, so it makes sense to the audience."*

I'm pretty sure I broke some kind of record for being asked to 'say it again', but less... me. My favourite?

*"Can you say that again but with a bit more... tension?"*

What does that even mean? More tension? Like a pulled hamstring?

Vox Pops weren't about capturing reality. They were about weaponising your own words against you - stripped of tone, timing, and context - then repackaging them to support whatever storyline they were pushing that week.

They don't need a script when they can just script you.

## SACRIFICING EVE

They act like the Vox Pop is sacred. Like stepping into a Catholic confessional - private, protected, just you and your truth.

Bullshit.

Me and Orton did ours right in front of each other on the honeymoon. No privacy. Just performance.

But when they needed to sacrifice someone, the Vox Pops suddenly became something else - a confessional turned courtroom. And Melinda -the bobble-headed expert with all the false authority of a YouTube life coach - didn't just nod along. She flat-out declared Eve had lied. Publicly. With conviction. Like her word was law.

And for a moment, I betrayed my own judgement.

Even I believed it.

I'll never forget the look on Eve's face at her last commitment ceremony -devastated, blindsided. The kind of pain that hits when you realise you were never going to be protected. And when she said goodbye to me - distant, hollow, already half-vanished - it haunted me for a long time after.

She didn't lie.

They just needed someone to burn.

And Melinda lit the match.

## THE WAKE-UP CALL

I had visions, in the beginning. Of looking composed. Glowing. Maybe even iconic. I imagined stepping in front of the cameras with soft glam, a killer outfit, giving effortless screen presence. Instead, I got woken up like I was late for a fire drill.

The reality was junior producers tapping at my door at an ungodly hour, whispering like we were in a hostage situation - "Hey babe, just a quick Vox when you're ready" - as if that made it gentler. Half the time I opened the door with my head scarf still on and yesterday's thoughts stuck to my face.

Between the endless filming, the emotional whiplash, and the sheer unpredictability of whatever scene they were trying to squeeze out of me, looking good was no longer the goal. Survival was. Vanity gave up and left the chat by day three.

By the time they dragged me out of bed for the fifth early morning in a row, I wasn't thinking about my angles-the glam squad in my head had been replaced by pure wine and survival instinct. I didn't care what I looked like anymore. I just didn't want to cry on camera *before* breakfast.

There's nothing more violating than being half-asleep in a foreign flat, in a fake marriage, and having someone knock on your door at 6am like hotel room service from hell. They'd march in, draw the curtains, demand you get up. Naturally? I hadn't even peed yet.

## RELIEVED OF DUTY

By my second - and final - week, the poor things had started to give up. They'd realised dragging me out of bed, slapping on a mic, and coaxing a storyline out of my eyebags just wasn't worth the hassle. I wasn't giving fairytale; I was giving fed up. The cost-to-chaos ratio had dipped. Badly. I was a woman powered by alcohol, contempt, and contractual obligation. At some point, they must've realised the juice wasn't worth the squeeze.

When they finally steered him toward someone new, someone more pliable, more willing to perform, it was the first time I truly exhaled. I encouraged it. I didn't care. I just let them redirect the cameras, the chaos, and the hand holding.

He had no direction of his own. He just clung to whatever was nearest, hoping it would drag him somewhere worth arriving. So, I knew the moment I let go of his hand, he'd show himself. No script to follow, no one to mimic - just him, unfiltered. And sure enough, he didn't walk forward. He flailed. Without me steadying the frame, the illusion couldn't hold. They didn't need me to say a word. He was writing the narrative all by himself now and just like that, they had their next storyline.

And thank God. It wasn't vindication. It wasn't even peace. It was a quiet extraction-like being smuggled out of a hostage situation with no fanfare and bad lighting.

I didn't get a happy ending. But I did get the next best thing: irrelevance and in reality TV, that's practically witness protection.

## THE FINAL INSULT

And somehow - *somehow* - after *everything,* they still forced an edit to make *me* look like the problem. Not the man crying on loop about a six-year-old breakup while I politely disassociated over tropical fruit. Not the man who casually brought his baggage, and his 'secret', down the aisle like it was a plus-one.

No, it was *me* - the woman who didn't clap, sob, or coddle on cue - who got served up as the nation's villain.

A week of forced connection, recycled trauma, and undercooked food in brown cardboard boxes, turned into a highlight reel of my "bad attitude." No context. No compassion. Just a carefully curated pile of harsh words, silences, and split-second reactions that the public would eat alive.

It seems that the worst thing you can do on reality TV isn't lying, or oversharing, or even risking someone's health. It's having boundaries. God forbid you don't fake a fairytale. If you won't perform the love story, they'll rewrite you as the villain.

Roll credits. Cue the hate.

## CONTENT OVER CARE

They were young, these overly keen producers -hovering around ready to draw back your curtains and drag you out of bed. I felt like Goldie Hawn in *Private Benjamin,* except instead of the army, it was a less than luxury serviced apartment with our names stuck on a plaque on the apartment door- filled of broken dreams and ring lights. To top it off, a wedding photo placed on the table so unflattering it looked like a crime scene still - two strangers caught mid-regret, stuffed into a frame that looked like it came free with petrol.

They hung around watching like hawks full of fake empathy like it was part of their uniform. They'd ask if you were okay with tilted heads, but the moment you hesitated - really hesitated - you'd see the flicker of panic. Not because they cared but because it might delay the schedule. Their job wasn't to support you; it was to get you on set, on time, looking camera-ready, even if you were one panic attack away from the floor or one delusional monologue away from jumping off a ledge. Their concern was performative, transactional. Sympathy with a stopwatch. You could be shaking, crying, visibly unravelling, and they'd still gently steer you toward the camera, whispering, "We're just heading to mic you now," like that would fix everything. Then they'd disappear, relieved you didn't crack all over their precious call sheet.

## UNSCRIPTED AND UNCOOPERATIVE

To be fair, I didn't make their lives easy. I was such an amateur, I probably made them question their career choices daily. I didn't hit my marks, I asked too many questions, and I had the audacity to want context before being filmed squirming in discomfort. While other cast members strutted in like they'd studied at the Stanislavski School of Fake Crying, I was still figuring out where to look when someone said "action." I wasn't media trained; I was just traumatised. Which, it became clear is much harder to direct.

Honestly, the regular producers looked just as tired and fed up as I felt. You could see it in their eyes: even they were exhausted by the tragedy they were being paid to capture. It was like we were all trapped in the same mess, just playing different roles in a show, no one really believed in anymore.

After my last commitment to camera, I was done. No more interviews. No more setups. No more smiling on cue while the walls closed in. I packed my things in silence and made my way home with the kind of stillness you only feel after surviving something you're not even ready to name. It didn't feel like I'd wrapped filming - it felt like I'd been freed from a trafficking ring. The difference between reality TV and captivity, at that point, was just paperwork.

I'm sure they were thrilled to see the back of me. I'd drained their patience, wrecked their narrative arcs, and refused to smile sweetly while being served nonsense. They must rue the day they cast me. They thought they were getting a bride; they got a liability with a sharp tongue and working Wi-Fi. Sometimes I wonder if they clocked it - realised I wasn't just difficult, I was dangerous. I'd seen through the whole performance: the fake empathy, the pre-baked drama, the crocodile concern. Once you spot the strings, it's only a matter of time before you start pulling them.

## THE CUT THAT CUTS DEEP

Editing is where the real storytelling happens in reality TV and where the truth goes to die. You can live a whole experience, raw and unpredictable, but once it hits the cutting room floor, you're at the mercy of someone whose only goal is to make it entertaining. They're not storytellers. They're surgeons with scissors and a deadline, carving out a version of you that fits the show's agenda. If you cried once, you were unstable. If you snapped once, you were toxic. And if you dared to look bored, congratulations - you were "cold." Context? Gone. Nuance? Deleted. What's left is a Frankenstein version of yourself stitched together from your worst five seconds.

## THE FRANKENWHORE EDIT

They don't just cut for time-they cut for character. Your hours of footage become a jigsaw puzzle made of your worst expressions, most awkward pauses, and one-off remarks dragged out like personality traits. One throwaway comment can be stitched next to an entirely different scene and suddenly you're the ice queen, the bitch, the narcissist. Forget linear storytelling-this is emotional collage. They'll splice a scene from day three with footage from day ten, drop in a close-up of someone looking disgusted, and voilà-conflict. Continuity? Who cares. All that matters is making you digestible and dramatic.

At one commitment ceremony, while I was speaking about something entirely unrelated, P-Dawg Brut thrust his fists in the air and suddenly hit me with, "But the uh uh is good, yea?"-a sexually loaded comment that came out of nowhere. It was so out of place, I laughed in discomfort and didn't even answer. What could I say? It wasn't a question-it was bait. A scripted prompt, thrown in to try and lure me into playing the role they'd already cast in their heads. They weren't trying to understand me - they were trying to corner me. At least that's how it felt to me at the time. And the version of me they wanted was simple: the oversexed, older woman. The OAP whore. That was the storyline they were determined to squeeze me into.

## GOOD TV = BAD FAITH

They weaponise silence. They reassign reactions. Someone could be laughing at a joke off-camera, and it'll be cut to look like they're laughing at your pain. You could be pausing to think, and they'll throw in suspense music like you're hiding something. And voiceovers? Pure evil. You might've said something completely innocent and weeks prior, but they'll slap it over a tense moment to imply you're calculated or cruel. It's not editing, it's emotional manipulation in surround sound.

## THEY KNEW WHAT THEY WERE DOING

Every show has its roles: the sweetheart, the underdog, the hot mess, the villain. If you're not slotting neatly into one, don't worry - they'll force you in. You can feel it happening as you're filmed - how the producers fish for certain reactions, how they ask the same question ten different ways until you say something they can use. But when you don't play along? They'll take whatever crumbs you give and edit them into the version of you that best fits their plot. They're not capturing reality; they're confirming their pitch deck.

## YOU DON'T GET A SAY -YOU GET AN ARC

You might think you're coming onto a show to be yourself. Cute. What you get is a "journey" - but not one you chose. The editors decide your beginning, middle and end before you've even unpacked your bags. If they want your arc to be "girl unravels," then buckle up because no amount of calm, rational behaviour will save you. They'll cut those parts. Your whole personality is reduced to a three-act structure: Enter. Cry. Exit. And if you dare to challenge it afterwards? You're "bitter" or "can't take the heat."

## POST-PRODUCTION PUPPETRY

This is where the magic (read: damage) happens. Music cues tell the audience how to feel: sinister strings for your side-eye, whimsical flutes for someone else's delusion. Dramatic zooms on reactions that weren't even in the same room. Slow-mo on your worst facial expression. They craft mood like a thriller director and pathologise emotion like they've got a psychology degree. You're not just being edited, you're being puppeteered. And the audience? They're so dazzled by the drama they never notice the strings.

## WHO CAN BLAME THE AUDIENCE?

Who can blame them? The audience isn't there to dissect every edit or pause to wonder, "Was that reaction even from the same scene?" They're watching for entertainment, not forensic analysis. They trust what's on screen because that's the whole point of television: to feel something without having to question its architecture. They're not evil, they're engrossed. They don't see the strings; they see the story - and I was written as a story. It's easy to judge when you're handed a curated version of someone, one clip at a time, edited for outrage and sprinkled with ominous music.

The real issue isn't that viewers believed it, it's that the people who made it *wanted* them to. They *bank* on that belief. They rely on our collective willingness to take what we see at face value, to root for the hero, hate the villain, and move on to the next episode.

## CHARACTER ASSASSINATION, WITH COMMERCIAL BREAKS

In the end, they didn't just edit the footage - they edited *me*. They trimmed away empathy, context, humour, exhaustion, hesitation - everything that made me remotely human. They cherry-picked my sharpest moments, looped my silences like they meant malice, and stitched together a woman so cold she could refrigerate a wine cellar. A woman the public could hate without flinching. The version of me shown on screen felt like a character. She wasn't real. She was a storyline.

The audience weren't there to question camera angles or continuity. They wanted to be entertained, and I gave them what the producers wanted them to see: a pantomime villain in a designer dress. They didn't see the rain-soaked picnics, the hours of emotional labour, the quiet endurance. They saw the cut eye. The raised brow. The woman who didn't play nice.

I wasn't cast to be palatable - I was cast to provoke. So, when I didn't break down on cue or baby a man-child through his nightly cheating sob story, they decided I'd broken the rules. I wasn't soft enough. I wasn't grateful enough. I wasn't fake enough.

So, they cut the rest, kept the worst, and called it a personality.

And the nation swallowed it whole.[1]

1 Disclaimer: The events and experiences described in this chapter reflect the author's personal recollection and perspective. Some dialogue has been paraphrased, condensed, or altered for clarity. Names and identifying details have been changed or withheld to protect privacy. Interpretations of motives and behaviour are the author's own and based on how they were experienced at the time.

# CHAPTER 4:
# THE STD THEY HID FROM ME

## THE TRUTH I WASN'T MEANT TO KNOW

I wasn't meant to find out. I didn't set out to uncover any hidden truths. The revelation that my match was a health and safety risk wasn't the result of some investigation on my part. It was a chance discovery, something I stumbled upon purely by accident.

They claim that they test all of us. They claim the background checks are rigorous. You think you're going into a process where somebody has been vetted and is safe.

I wasn't even 100% sure of what I had found until the final commitment ceremony. That's when I confronted him, hissing under my breath, "*You even came in here with an STD*". His shocked reaction confirmed everything. His eyes snapped wide - that kind of jolt only pure panic delivers. He didn't deny it. Didn't speak. Just stared into space like he was trying to leave his own body. And that was it. He sat frozen for the remainder of the commitment ceremony, like the air had been sucked out of the room - or at least out of him.

## PIGLET: MY PASTEL-COLOURED PRISON

Retreat Week: I'd been bundled onto a coach. They called it a party bus, but there were no party favours, no music, no vibe. Just one of the cast members strumming a ukulele like we were on a school trip to hell.

I had no idea where we were going. After being denied access to the so-called experts, I was on that coach for hours, with no clue, signal, or dignity, just dragged along to the retreat week like a prop they weren't finished using.

To top it off, the most insufferable, pick-me welfare producer with a perm, they could find clutched my phone like it was state property and refused to hand it over, saying she'd checked with the execs - and they said no. Basic contact with my own life was something I needed permission for.

## CONTROLLED, CONTAINED, AND CUT OFF

Maybe that's the real reason they take our personal phones away. Not just for filming continuity or to keep us "present in the process" - their favourite excuse - but to cut off our contact with the outside world. So that when you realise you've been stitched up, you can't call a friend, you can't message your sister, you can't even Google what the hell is going on. You're trapped. Surrounded by cameras, controlled by producers, with no lifeline back to reality. And that's exactly how they want it.

When you do finally get your phone back - for five whole minutes if you're lucky - they sit in on the call. Hovering. Eavesdropping, just in case you try to form an independent thought. I remember asking to use mine on my daughter's birthday. They made it seem like an enormous ask. When they did finally hand it over, I refused to give it back. I'd been forced to wait the whole day to speak to my child.

A junior welfare producer - bless him, fresh out of drama school or trauma school, who knows - started positioning himself to wrestle it from under my clothes. I said, "Go on. I dare you." I was feral. I meant it. There are maternal instincts, and then there's the unhinged wrath of a mother trapped in a Network 4 social experiment.

## THE LUXURY OF CONTAINMENT

This "welfare producer" was way out of his depth - a kid playing lifeguard in a rip current. He tried to pacify me by waving his hand around the cabin - Piglet, it was called, ironically - and said something like, "Look, you're in luxury. Freestanding bath and everything." As if a bathtub was going to rinse off the psychological abuse. When that didn't work (shockingly), he panicked and called in the big guns - the ultimate welfare producer, the head honcho, the one they save for full meltdowns. She sat silently beside me (eavesdropping, of course) while I finally made my calls.

## WHEN THE STAR TURN DOESN'T LAND

Meanwhile, next door, Orton was filming a monologue at a dinner party about how awful his wife was, because, clearly, the entire cast and crew needed to hear his pitiful performance piece.

Imagine that. I was out of the way; his moment had finally arrived. He stood up like he was accepting a lifetime achievement award (so I heard - I was locked in Piglet). Poured his heart out to the room, desperate for his standing ovation.

The best part? The whole speech got binned in the edit. Not even the producers thought it was worth airtime.

Funny, isn't it? He gave them everything - the speech, the spin, the fake sincerity - and it still wasn't good enough. That's the currency of this machine: usefulness. If you're not dramatic, desirable, or deranged, then you're disposable. His big moment, his emotional climax, didn't make the cut. Even manufactured martyrdom must hit the right beat.

## CONSENT WITHOUT CLARITY

This is what they call "informed consent." It was a signature on a contract waved around like a moral shield, but consent under coercion isn't consent - not when information is withheld. Not when you're isolated, gaslit, and manipulated for entertainment. They knew what they were doing. They knew what he had, and they still matched us. They still filmed it. They still fed it to the public. Once you've signed, you're not a person anymore. Now you're a storyline.

The only thing you're consenting to is being used. And possibly even being sued.

## CLEAN TEST, DIRTY EDIT

I didn't intend to drag his diagnosis into daylight but then, I didn't intend to be handed to him either. But as he showed me - and as this whole twisted process made clear - it's a cruel world. So let me return the favour.

I wasn't afforded dignity. I wasn't given protection, or truth, or even the bare minimum of care. What I got was collusion, spin, and the full force of a machine that feeds on humiliation. And him? He lied. Over and over. So, no - I won't protect the people who never once protected me.

They let it happen. They wrapped it in silence, sealed it with a contract, and called it television. They chose the storyline over my safety, the ratings over my reality. In their world, it's easier to let a woman take the fall than to hold a man accountable, especially one delivering deceit on cue.

Did I catch it? No. But I did not escape the consequences. He came in infectious. Not just medically, but morally and I left carrying the stigma, the silence, and the mess he made.

The same mess I'm now tidying up.

You're welcome, "hubby".

## VOILA, BITCHES

They didn't say it to reassure me; they said it to shut me up. "*The press won't report this.*" A warning, not a comfort. This was their way of saying: you're powerless, you'll vanish like all the others. This is how they operate - bury the harm, protect the show. Spin the truth until it's unrecognisable, then hand you the damage and call it your story. There's nothing accidental about it. It's a cold, calculated system that thrives on silence and banks on you breaking down quietly.

My last words to them were "I'll find a way".

Here it is.

Voila.[1]

---

1 Disclaimer: The events and experiences described in this chapter reflect the author's personal recollection and perspective. Some dialogue has been paraphrased, condensed, or altered for clarity. Names and identifying details have been changed or withheld to protect privacy. Interpretations of motives and behaviour are the author's own and based on how they were experienced at the time.

# CHAPTER 5:
# THE PILE ON

## WHEN THE INTERNET LOSES ITS MIND

I didn't know the hate had started. I wasn't watching the show at the same time as everyone else, I wasn't checking social media - I was talking to one friend on the phone blissfully unaware saying, "I think it's all fine. I didn't say anything bad". Famous last words.

Then I checked my Instagram. The comments were turned off.

I hadn't turned them off. Truth be told, I didn't even know how.

I called my friend who was managing my socials and when she answered, her voice sounded as if she'd just come back from Chernobyl. Quiet. Shell-shocked. She said, "*I had to turn them off.*" But she hadn't warned me. She hadn't even texted. She was overwhelmed.

The tone of the hate. It wasn't just angry. It was emotional. Personal. Like I'd broken into their house and slapped their nan. People were furious - genuinely furious - that I didn't like this man they'd watched on TV for about four and a half minutes.

*"How dare she."*

How dare she not fall in love with him?

How dare she not want to spend her honeymoon watching him cry over an imaginary ex?

How dare she not appreciate his head-shaking and vague statements about being an engineer-slash-actor?

It wasn't a critique. It was possession. Like I'd messed with their imaginary boyfriend, and they were coming for blood.

## TROLLS, BOTS AND OTHER MYSTICAL CREATURES

That night, I turned the comments back on, and it felt like stepping into a digital uncanny valley. The messages were eerily uniform, with identical phrasing, punctuation, and a peculiar fixation on the word "vile." It was as if a single, uncreative entity had mass-produced these insults, deploying them through a fleet of faceless profiles.

I had braced for the usual social media circus of pitchforks, fire emojis, and a casual death threat sprinkled in, but what I found was weirder. The hate felt... recycled. Same insult, same phrasing, same weird obsession with "vile". It was like someone with too much time, and a lot of hate in their heart had drafted the world's most uninspired hate speech and just ctrl + V-ed it into the void - over and over again, like a budget bot with no imagination. I wasn't being trolled. I was being spammed.

## BOTS OR NOT: THE DIGITAL ROAST

This led me to a disconcerting question: **Do reality shows employ bots to sustain their narratives?** The idea isn't far-fetched. In fact, Netflix's *The Circle* Season 6 introduced "Max," an AI chatbot designed to masquerade as a human contestant. Max engaged with other players through a simulated social media platform, convincingly mimicking human interaction until producers revealed his true nature after a few episodes.

Moreover, the Spanish reality show *Deep Fake Love* took manipulation a step further by using deepfake technology to fabricate videos of contestants' partners engaging in infidelity. These doctored clips were presented to participants, blurring the line between reality and fabrication and eliciting genuine emotional turmoil.

Such instances highlight a troubling trend: the deliberate use of AI and bots in reality television to manipulate both participants and audiences. This not only questions the authenticity of the content but also raises ethical concerns about the psychological impact on those involved.

If this was organic, then humanity's worse off than I thought. And if it wasn't? Then it's even darker than I imagined.

## INVASION OF THE KEYBOARD WARRIORS

I started replying to the keystone keyboard warriors. Nothing aggressive - no caps lock, no name-calling, no rage. Just calm, direct questions. The sort of tone that really unnerves people because it suggests you're not broken - you're awake. Some ghosted faster than my ex after "I'm pregnant" as a joke. You'd think after all the venom they'd spewed, they'd be foaming at the mouth, ready to double down. But most of them vanished.

That's the thing about keyboard warriors. They've got all the bravado of a pit bull online and the emotional stability of a damp flannel in real life. They're gladiators in the comments and ghosts in the inbox. Big talkers behind an anime avatar and a username like @truthbombz_47, but ask them a basic question like, "Why do you care so much about a stranger's edit on a reality show?" and suddenly it's tumbleweeds and profile deactivations.

Most of them couldn't argue their way out of a paper bag. They rely on groupthink, hashtags, and the false courage that comes from typing in the dark with a digestive biscuit in one hand and zero accountability in the other. The second you respond with logic - or worse, humour - they malfunction. It's like showing a vampire a mirror. Poof. Gone.

And I thought, hang on a minute. *You* came onto *my* page to insult *me*, but now that I've got something to say, you've gone mute? What is this? Drive-by abuse followed by witness protection? Either these are bots, or they're the type of people who throw a punch and then sprint off like they've just egged a house and heard a police siren. It was like confronting a school bully and watching them reverse-evolve into a hedgehog.

They had the energy of someone who yells "slag!" from a moving car, but the moment you catch up at the traffic lights, they're suddenly fascinated by the glove compartment. All bark, no spine, powered entirely by Wi-Fi and pineapple juice. You could practically hear their keyboards seize up the second they realised I wasn't going to cry or crumble. I was going to reply calmly, grammatically, and with better punctuation than they'd ever seen in their lives. That, apparently, was the real violence.

That's when it clicked: half these people don't want a conversation - they want a cartoon villain. A punchbag. Someone they can dump their daily rage onto between snack breaks and scrolling. They don't see you as a person; they see a character built from dodgy editing, bad lighting, and their own unresolved issues.

When you reply like a real human, calm and coherent, not frothing at the mouth, it short-circuits the whole performance. You break the spell. And just like that, *poof*, they disappear.

But then, I had to ask myself again: were they even real people? Or just a swarm of bots set loose to maintain the narrative? Because when you break the spell and engage them like a human being, they turn into Houdini.

It turns out the one thing these people fear more than a "toxic woman" is a woman who answers back with full emotions and no shame.

## THE GIRL WHO DROVE HIM TO THE BRINK

This is where it tipped into full-blown parody.

By not falling in love with a man I'd known for five minutes (on national TV), I was now single-handedly endangering the mental health of the entire male population. Forget global warming - *this* was the real crisis. Suddenly, I wasn't just edited as difficult. I was being framed as some kind of psychological terrorist. An emotional sniper. A one-woman epidemic. Men I'd never met were having their feelings projected onto my footage, and somehow, *their* stability was now *my* responsibility.

Meanwhile, the man in question? Lying was his full-time job. Faking roles, faking businesses, faking entire life stories with the confidence of a man who'd watched one too many IG business coach reels on personal branding. Oh, and let's not forget the actual, literal health risk he didn't bother to mention. But no, let's all rally around *him*. Let's cradle his ego in cashmere while torching the woman who didn't clap for the performance.

Evidently, refusing to stroke a man's delusions is now considered radical feminism. Telling a man he's not worth shit? That's no longer a personal boundary. It's an act of war. I wasn't challenging one man. I was seemingly bringing down the entire patriarchy with my facial expressions. A nation of men in crisis because I said, "I'm good, thanks."

## CLUELESS

The truth is that the viewers didn't know what they weren't shown. They didn't see the lies. They didn't see the moments we laughed or when I was just trying to get through it without losing my mind. They didn't see the biohazard. So, how mad can I really be at them? They weren't watching reality. They were watching a hit job.

If all you're fed is the villain edit, then yeah you're gonna boo. They didn't edit me to be understood. They edited me to be hated. And it worked.

There's something deeply unsettling about how quickly people rush to protect the man, especially on shows like this. It's like the audience has been trained to see him as the default victim, even when the facts say otherwise. Just as quickly, they turn on the woman. Especially if she doesn't behave how they expect. If she challenges him. Questions the narrative. Refuses to play nice.

We've all been taught to root for the person who seems more "vulnerable," and reality TV knows exactly how to exploit that. They know that a woman standing her ground can be edited into arrogance. That doubt can be spun into cruelty. That not smiling through discomfort makes you cold. Hostile. Problematic.

That's what the show counted on. Not just outrage but participation. They didn't need to convince everyone I was the villain. They just needed enough people to go, *"Yeah, she's a bit much"*. The show relied on women joining in hating me - not despite being women, but *because* they were women.

## YOUNG, INDEPENDENT, AND UNAPOLOGETIC

There was one thing that stood out like a flare in the madness. My daughter's TikTok - mostly Gen Z and younger millennials girls- were supportive, sharp, dare I say it, in awe. They didn't just *watch* the show, they *read* it. They saw through the dodgy edit, spotted the manipulations, and called them out in real-time.

Turns out, those "addicted" screens have taught them a thing or two about how stories are shaped and whose side they're supposed to be on.

They know how audio can be lifted, scenes rearranged, context stripped. They've grown up online, watching influencers curate realities, and they bring that scepticism to everything they consume. They *get* that a show like this isn't a documentary - it's a storyline in search of a scapegoat.

Meanwhile, the older crowd - the ones who accuse young people of being too sensitive - were losing their minds in the comments. Outraged. Foaming. Grasping for moral authority like it was a national sport. The real media literacy gap isn't about age, it's about who's willing to admit they're being played.

## FACEBOOK AND X/TWITTER: THE AMATEUR DETECTIVE AGENCY

Not content with just hurling insults, viewers went full Sherlock on what they thought were my company accounts, combing through every line like it held the secrets of the universe. Plot twist: it wasn't even my company. They wasted hours in their digital spy thriller, scrutinising someone else's financials. Imagine the dedication! All that time and effort just to get the wrong tea. You almost have to admire the commitment to being completely, hilariously mistaken.

Facebook. The land of big fonts, Daily Mail links, and middle-aged women called Mogda who wear their dressing gowns to the corner shop. That's where the real venom lived. These women didn't just dislike me - they *needed* to. You could feel it. Like I had walked into their house and laughed at their Live, Laugh, Love sign. They weren't just angry on behalf of this man; they were spiritually connected to him.

Honestly, most of them looked like they'd been arguing with customer service since 1998. Frumpy, furious, and dressed like a bad mood. The kind of women who should've been at home cooking toad in the hole, but instead were online, typing with one finger and rage-scrolling through my Instagram like I owed them rent.

These must be the kind of women I watch on *Love Rats,* scammed out of their savings because some bloke said his dog had cancer and couldn't afford the chemo. They'll fall for anything a man says as long as he says it with a straight face and a sob story.

So maybe it *is* generational. Perhaps younger women are more attuned to red flags and less invested in defending men they don't know. Presumably the older generation have been so conditioned to perform niceness and tolerate bullshit, they see any woman who refuses as dangerous. They don't like seeing women not putting up with suffering the way they have. Either way, I became the vessel for all their unresolved projection. And I didn't even get a sausage out of it.

## THE GENERATION THAT DOESN'T SETTLE

It's no accident that younger women today are walking out of relationships their mothers would've stayed in for decades - and doing it without a shred of apology. Gen Z and Millennial women are, statistically and psychologically, more independent than the generations before them. And it shows.

Marriage? Not the end goal. According to the stats, younger women are delaying it, ditching it, or redefining it entirely. They're getting degrees, building careers, and shockingly thriving without a ring on their finger. The horror.

Financially, they're earning their own money, paying their own rent, and not waiting for a man to "provide." Emotionally, they're just as self-sufficient. They've got therapy, group chats, and TikToks telling them they don't have to settle for crumbs.

They've also burned the handbook on traditional gender roles. Studies show they're far less likely to tolerate the "he provides, she nurtures" dynamic. In fact, if he can't communicate, cook, or clean, he's gone. No long-winded breakup letters. Just a blocked number and a curated soft-launch of their new era.

Younger women expect equality, emotional intelligence, and effort. And if they don't get it? They leave. Because independence isn't just about having your own money - it's about knowing your worth and refusing to negotiate it. Older generations might call that selfish. The rest of us call it evolution.

## STILL TRYING TO MAKE 'GRATEFUL WIFE' HAPPEN

Given this insight, it highlights just how laughably out of touch reality TV still is - clinging to some archaic formula where a woman's happy ending is only valid if it involves a man, a dress, and a group of strangers cheering her on like she's won the lottery. Shows like *Married at First Sight* are still trying to sell the idea that marriage is the ultimate prize, and that women should be grateful - grateful! - for any match handed to them, no matter how unsuitable. It's not just outdated. It's insulting. Especially when entire generations of women have already moved on from that narrative and are building lives that don't revolve around male approval or romantic success. The show isn't just behind the times, it's practically fossilised.

And yet, there I was - educated, independent, and self-sufficient - being cast in a role written decades ago. The strong woman who just needed to be "softened." The one who should be grateful she was matched at all. The producers didn't just ignore the progress women have made-they actively rewrote it. They weren't interested in who I actually was; they wanted a storyline. A spectacle. And if that meant shoving me into a mould that didn't fit, too bad. My independence wasn't a strength in their eyes - it was a problem to be edited, ridiculed, and ultimately punished. Because heaven forbid a woman on reality TV shows up knowing her worth and refusing to play the game.

## VILE TO SOME, GLOWING TO OTHERS

Then there were the DMs. In the middle of the digital witch hunt, there were these little gems. DMs from girls who somehow missed the memo that I was public enemy number one. "Babe, where did you get your earrings?" "What's your skincare routine?' Meanwhile, I'm drowning in a sea of vitriol. I've got one person telling me I'm a witch from hell and another asking if I can share my favourite serum and I'm sitting there thinking "Honey I can't even see my earrings through the smoke of this dumpster fire." To be honest, I respect her priorities.

It was surreal. Like giving a TED Talk during a house fire and someone still raises their hand to ask where your shoes are from.

## WHEN THE MADNESS TURNED INTO COMEDY

By the time it all properly descended into madness, my friends and I gave up trying to fix it and started treating it like performance art. The hate wasn't just loud, it was *operatic*. So, we leaned in. We embraced the full pantomime. If they were going to cast me as the villain, I may as well give them the show: big red dress, dramatic lighting, slow walk into frame. I wasn't Richelle anymore - I was *The Problem*™.

There was one night - and I swear this lives in my memory like an Oscar clip - Janey, drained from all the chaos, mentally preparing for another round of online abuse, asked me with the gravitas of someone waiting for a clinical diagnosis, "What's coming on tonight's episode?"

I said, with all the calm of a woman preparing for her own televised execution, "It's the episode where I say he's not a leader."

Like a Shakespearean widow hearing the kingdom had fallen, Janey cried into the phone, "Oh *nooooooooo*".

I was in bed, middle of the night, tears streaming. Not from despair. From hysterics. The internet was calling me vile, abusive, the root of all male suffering, yet I was doubled over, shaking, crying with laughter, as Janey's voice played in my head like a West End ghost: "Oh *nooooooooo.*" It was surreal. Hilarious. Like being publicly stoned with emojis while your best friend provides the soundtrack.

And that's the thing. While strangers were dissecting my personality like a dead frog in a GCSE science class, I was in bed, howling with laughter over Janey's tragic wailing. Not because I wasn't affected, but because by that point, what else was left? You either break down, or you take the piss. And I picked the piss.

They called me toxic. Unhinged. Everything wrong with women today.

And I thought - if refusing to play nice while being lied to, stitched up, and offered to the public like reality TV roadkill makes me toxic, then fine. Pass the label maker.

Somewhere between the death threats, the women defending a man they didn't know, and the endless comments typed from grease-stained kitchens, I found a strange calm. Not closure. Not justice.

Just peace. And a pair of earrings that survived the war.

## REFLECTIONS ON THE DRAMA MACHINE

Looking back, I'm acutely aware that my time on the show was relatively brief. In the grand scheme of reality TV, I was just another fleeting character. Yet, the production team had a singular goal: to make every moment I was on screen as sensational as possible.

In the early episodes, the edit was laser-focused on creating as much drama and discourse as possible to hook viewers. Since my time on screen was short, they couldn't fully develop the nuances of my "marriage". Instead, they aimed to make my portrayal as impactful and sensational as possible.

In acknowledging this, I find a strange sort of peace. Understanding the mechanics of the reality TV machine doesn't excuse the harm, but it does help me separate my true self from the character they created. My hope is that by sharing this reflection, others who watch these shows might pause and remember that behind every dramatic edit is a person whose story is far more complex.

I understand that reality TV thrives on drama. Producers and editors are tasked with crafting narratives that grip viewers, often at the expense of the real people behind the scenes. While I could have lived with a "villain edit" as part of the show's formula, the way they concealed his diagnosis and how they treated me made it unforgivable.

The brief time I was on TV was magnified into a spectacle, one that didn't reflect the whole truth of who I am. The edit may have made for compelling television, but it also reduced my experience to a caricature, leaving a skewed version of me in the minds of viewers.

What's even more striking is how a few hours of filming can be manipulated into a narrative that is so far removed from the truth, concealing significant points that could have helped viewers understand my reactions. I'm not perfect, and I don't claim to be - no one is. But did I deserve that level of distortion? No.

In an ironic twist, my "match" was there to propel his acting career, hoping for a breakout role. Yet, somehow, I ended up being the main character of our coupling. Life sure has a sense of humour, casting me in the spotlight while he played a supporting role in what was supposed to be his big break. The universe sure has a funny way of flipping the script!

He must've been *really* desperate for airtime. Most people, when faced with a diagnosis dilemma like that, might rethink going on national TV to find a wife. He saw it as character development. The kind of delusion you need to frame a public health risk as a career move? That's not ambition - that's pathology.

## FOR THE WOMEN WHO KNEW BETTER

In the end, after all the chaos and all the noise, it came down to something simple: just peace and a skincare routine that stayed loyal during the onslaught. It was a reminder that even in the darkest times, there are small treasures that endure. And speaking of treasures, I'd be remiss not to mention the people who helped me through it all - my followers. Those who followed me *because* of the madness, not in spite of it. The ones who saw the edit, the chaos, the pile-on and still thought, "No, something's not adding up."

I have so much love for you. The women I'm aligned with. No performance. No pretending. Just instinct. Sharp eyes. And, probably, exquisite earrings.

# CHAPTER 6:
# WOMEN UNDER THE LENS

## THE GENDERED EDIT

Reality TV loves its female archetypes. There's always the "crazy one", the "ice queen", the "slut", and the "pick-me." It's practically a casting requirement. Meanwhile, the men are allowed to be "flawed", "misunderstood", or "on a journey". It's not just lazy editing - it's a mirror held up to how society still processes women: through reduction, distortion, and double standards. This chapter is about what happens when you become one of those characters - and how easy it is for the world to believe it.

## THE DOUBLE STANDARD IS THE POINT

This isn't about who got a "bad edit." It's about how quickly women are punished for being anything other than agreeable. Speak up and you're difficult. Set boundaries and you're controlling. Show emotion and you're unstable. Meanwhile, the men get nuance and forgiveness. They get to be "on a journey". Their flaws are humanised while women's are broadcast and framed in slow motion with ominous music.

The worst part is that it *worked.* Not just on the audience but on us too. When you're handed a version of yourself that's been cut and coloured to make you unrecognisable, you start to question your own instincts. You know what really happened, but still you catch yourself wondering if you *were* too harsh. Too much. Too *something.*

If I'd watched my edit without living it I might have judged me too. That's the real danger of the lens. It doesn't just warp how others see you; it chips away at your own reflection until even *you* start to believe the fiction.

## THE FALLOUT IS REAL

Once that version of you is out there, there's no taking it back. It doesn't matter what really happened. What matters is what they saw. What they were told to believe. When that belief solidifies, it spreads. The edit lives on in tweets, headlines, gossip threads, and group chats. Suddenly, you're not just managing your reality, you're defending yourself against a version of you that you never chose.

This isn't just frustrating - it's dangerous. Women who get edited into these roles are thrown to the wolves. The online backlash isn't about plotlines; it's deeply personal. Every outfit, every reaction, every facial expression is picked apart. The toll is real. All because someone in a control room decided you were the week's antagonist.

## WHEN WOMEN ENFORCE THE SCRIPT

There's something especially bleak about watching women drive this machine. Female producers, editors, and journalists who package these reductive stories and push them out as "content." They're just surviving in a system that rewards this kind of storytelling. Or maybe they've bought into the idea that this is what sells. Either way, it stinks. Because you want to believe that women will protect each other. But sometimes, they're the ones handing out the knives.

## POWER, BUT AT WHAT COST?

That's the paradox - women in these roles have power, but it's power with strings attached. They can shape narratives, but only within the framework that keeps women small, reactive, and consumable. So, the cycle continues. We applaud "strong female leads" in fiction, then tear real women to shreds on screen. The message is clear: be bold, but not *that* bold. Be visible, but not in your face. Be powerful, but only if it doesn't make anyone uncomfortable.

And if it does? Well, there's always a villain slot waiting to be filled.

## THE DOUBLE BIND OF BEING A BLACK WOMAN ON REALITY TV

## THE BIAS BEYOND THE SCREEN

A 2021 analysis by *The Guardian* found that Black women on UK reality shows are 83% more likely to end up in the bottom two of public votes. That's not a fluke - it's a pattern. And I got a front-row seat. The viewers didn't just dislike me - they went on a rage fuelled attack. They dug up employment details, targeted my job, and flooded my inbox with bile.

This isn't "criticism." It's a system doing exactly what it was built to do.

The Fawcett Society found that Black women receive 84% more abusive tweets than white women - with the abuse more likely to include both racial and gendered slurs. It's not feedback. It's targeted harassment, cloaked in "public opinion," fuelled by a storyline they were spoon-fed and an edit designed to provoke.

## STILL CONTROLLING THE STORYLINE

After my fourth episode aired, one of the other cast messaged me: "Riche, I haven't seen you laugh once." She said it with sadness - like even she was disturbed by the edit I was getting.

Later, in a post-show interview, she and another castmate tried to speak positively about me. But it never made it in. Someone - I don't know who - decided, *"We'll cut that. She doesn't want anything to do with the show."*

Because when you're a Black woman on reality TV, the story they choose for you isn't just edited - it's enforced. And if the edit says you're the villain, no one's allowed to say otherwise.

## WHEN STEREOTYPES DEFINE THE SCRIPT

Being a Black woman on UK reality TV isn't just a role, it's a trap. You're expected to fit into a script that was written long before you arrived: angry, fiery, confrontational - but never too complex, never too soft, never too human. If you dare to deviate from that script, you're punished. On screen. In headlines. In your DMs.

I lived it. I walked in with boundaries, confidence, and standards, and I watched as those qualities were twisted into something threatening. My assertiveness became 'aggression,' my silence became 'coldness', and my strength - something that should have been respected - became the excuse for a villain edit. Meanwhile, the man beside me got the benefit of the doubt, soft music, and endless empathy. That's not coincidence. That's the formula.

According to Ofcom's 2023 review of diversity in UK television, things are improving on paper - more faces of colour on screen, statistically speaking. But behind the camera? Black women are still some of the least represented in the rooms where the real decisions get made. The ones shaping the stories. And that absence shows. You feel it in how we're portrayed: rarely nuanced, often skewed.

The LSE Media Policy Project said it plainly in 2022 - Black women on UK reality TV are routinely edited into the same tired tropes: the angry Black woman, the difficult diva. Pick your poison. It's not storytelling, it's typecasting.

You don't need to be an industry insider to notice who gets protected and who gets punished. It's obvious in the edits, in the headlines, and in the silence that greets certain types of harm. Behind every "bad edit" is a system that's been studied, documented, and is still allowed to thrive.

I wasn't surprised. Not really. As a Black woman, I walked into a system that was never built for me - one that's quick to weaponise our strength, mock our confidence, and erase our softness. I knew the risks. I knew the history. I knew I could be reduced, rewritten, repackaged as a stereotype.

And I did it anyway.

It tried to break me but I'm still here. Still standing. Still telling the story they tried to rewrite.

That, in itself, is resistance.

## RACE. GENDER. POWER. ALL OF IT.

What happened to me isn't unique. It's structural. And until producers stop casting women as plot devices, until audiences stop measuring our worth against impossible standards, until the industry is forced to confront the racism embedded in its formulas, this will keep happening.

Looking back at my own experience, what struck me most was how predictably the gender roles were divided - and how aggressively the edit leaned into them. The women were boxed into extremes: too emotional, too cold, too desperate. Meanwhile, the men were given breathing room to be flawed, "working on themselves," and understood. I watched as strong, articulate women were reduced to caricatures while men skated by with far less scrutiny. Living through that made it impossible to ignore just how calculated and one-sided those portrayals really were. It wasn't just disappointing, it was deliberate.

## NOT BITTER - JUST AWARE

Let me be clear: this isn't about bitterness. It's not about score-settling or trying to rewrite public opinion. I'm not here to convince anyone to like me. I'm here to explore something bigger than one edit, one show, or one-character assassination.

What I experienced gave me something far more valuable than a temporary redemption arc - it gave me insight. A lived, embodied understanding of how women are framed, judged, and consumed in entertainment. How audiences, including other women, are nudged into predictable responses, and how powerful female voices are still seen as threats unless they're packaged just right.

I didn't set out to become a case study in gendered media narratives. But here I am, holding the evidence. While it was brutal to live through, it also gave me the language, and the nerve, to name what I saw.

So no, I'm not bitter. I'm informed.

When you've stood in the middle of a machine that profits from misrepresentation, when you've seen the edits, the omissions, the twisting of truth, you stop asking for sympathy and start asking better questions. Who benefits when women are turned against each other? Why is a woman's strength edited out while her silence is spotlighted? What do we lose when we only tell half the story?

This book isn't about revenge. It's about reality - the kind you don't see on screen.

## BREAKING THE CYCLE
## WHY WOMEN HATE THE CONFIDENT WOMAN - AND LOVE THE UNDERDOG

It's one of the great ironies of reality TV: confident, self-assured women - women who know who they are and what they want - are often the ones who receive the most vitriol... from other women. Meanwhile, the "underdog" woman - the one who's more passive, quiet, or emotionally dependent - gets swarmed with support. It's not because she's weak, but because she's familiar. Comfortable. Safe. Confident women can be triggering because they force others to confront what they've suppressed, whether it's their own desires, fears, or untapped potential. If a woman sees someone embodying the freedom or power she was told to shrink from, it might not feel inspiring. It might feel like a personal failure.

This isn't about women being "jealous" of other women. That's lazy and convenient. It's deeper than that. Women are conditioned from a young age to compete for approval from men, teachers, peers, or the public. We're taught to keep our ambitions subtle and our confidence palatable. So, when a woman shows up on screen with boundaries, certainty, and a refusal to grovel for acceptance, she triggers something uncomfortable. Not just in men but in women, too.

Psychologists call this internalised misogyny: the unconscious adoption of sexist attitudes toward women by women themselves. It's what leads audiences to label assertive women as "cold" or "manipulative," while describing submissive women as "sweet" or "genuine" -even when the facts tell a different story. In reality TV, where editing is God and women are flattened into 'types,' this dynamic gets amplified to absurd levels.

Let's not undervalue how the edit encourages this. Viewers aren't reacting to the full picture; they're reacting to what they've been *socialised* to feel. Confident women are given ominous music. Their valid concerns are framed as overreactions. Their silences are weaponised. Meanwhile, the underdog is cued with soft piano and given space to tell sob stories. She gets empathy while the other gets outrage.

It's not just storytelling-it's social conditioning in real time.

Seeing it for what it is makes the damage impossible to ignore - and the need for fair, balanced representation for women all the more urgent.

Here's the real tragedy: when women tear down the woman with power, supposedly in defence of the underdog, they're not challenging the system - they're doing its job for it. That's not solidarity. That's self-sabotage dressed up as moral righteousness.

And the only winner is the machine that keeps us all small.

## WHY REPRESENTATION MATTERS - ESPECIALLY FOR YOUNG WOMEN

When you strip powerful women from a story - or worse, turn them into villains - you don't just flatten the narrative. You send a message. And for young female viewers, that message lands hard: don't be too loud. Don't be too ambitious. Don't stand up for yourself because you won't be liked.

Reality TV, like all media, holds a mirror up to culture. But it also shapes culture, so when that mirror only reflects petty conflict, insecurity, and dependency in women, it trains a generation to see those traits as normal - or even aspirational. It tells girls that being liked matters more important than being honest. It says that being desirable matters more than being respected. It reinforces that having a man is the goal, and everything else is background noise.

On the flip side, when young women see assertiveness without apology, boundaries without backlash, friendship without betrayal it changes them. It expands what they believe is possible. Studies show that media representation directly influences young people's self-esteem and sense of identity. Girls who see confident, multi-dimensional women on screen are more likely to see those qualities in themselves.

Powerful female representation doesn't mean perfection. It means complexity. It means giving women the space to be bold, wrong, kind, selfish, brilliant, messy - without punishing them for it. Without editing their strength into something sinister.

We had the potential to show that. We lived it. The women in my season were not caricatures or clichés, they were strong, young, ambitious women. We were each unique in our backgrounds, personalities, and reasons for being there. We supported each other. They argued at times, yes. But we also laughed. We respected each other and we held boundaries. At times, we doubted ourselves and each other. In other words, we were real. If the edit had honoured that instead of distorting it, it could have offered something powerful to the young women watching, but instead, the version they saw on-screen told them a different story - one that punished strength, rewarded submission, and reduced us to tropes.

We deserved better.

## WASTED POWER: HOW THE EDIT BETRAYED THE WOMEN IT COULD HAVE CELEBRATED

The producers had a goldmine. A cast full of women with brains, wit, boundaries, careers, style, bite - women who had survived things, built things, carried things. Women who could have *inspired* viewers. Who should have been framed as complex, strong, flawed, resilient human beings. But instead of choosing female empowerment, they chose the easier route: mockery, misrepresentation, and reduction.

The edit didn't celebrate strength, it punished it. Assertiveness was repackaged as aggression. Emotional honesty was spun as instability. Boundaries? Manipulated into selfishness or cruelty. If a woman spoke up, stood tall, refused to be walked over, the cameras kept rolling but she would be sliced down to size later in the editing room.

Meanwhile, men who stonewalled, deflected, or simply existed were handled with care. Given soft music. Second chances. A story arc. The same courtesies weren't extended to the women.

There was a chance to flip the script. To give viewers something richer than the usual "crazy woman vs poor man" template. Instead, the edit chose to reinforce everything reality TV is comfortable with: women tearing each other down, men being 'misunderstood,' and any woman who challenged the format becoming the villain in her own love story.

They didn't just miss the opportunity to showcase strong women. They actively buried it.

## THE COST OF BEING CAST

When you realise how calculated it all is - how every soundbite, every silence, every flash of emotion is manipulated to fit a narrative - it does something to your brain. You stop taking reactions at face value and start analysing everything. The edit doesn't just change how others see you; it changes how you see people. What started as a deeply personal experience slowly became something I began to study in real time, trying to make sense of the chaos with logic and observation.

This wasn't just reality TV - it was a masterclass in how women are shaped, silenced, and sold to the public. The edit didn't simply distort moments; it weaponised them. It took real women with real strength and complexity and flattened us into characters that fit a familiar and profitable script: the unhinged woman, the saintly man, the rivalry, the downfall. And audiences bought it because that's what they've been taught to expect.

But behind every manipulated scene was a choice. A choice to sideline truth in favour of spectacle. A choice to reward submission and punish resistance. A choice to turn power into a flaw.

Here's the uncomfortable question: is this just what women are supposed to expect when they sign up for reality TV?

Are we to expect we'll be cast as cautionary tales or emotional punching bags? That if we show confidence, we'll be cut down; if we show vulnerability, it'll be exploited; and if we dare to challenge the setup, we'll be presented to the public in a way designed to humiliate you. That the price of being visible is being vilified?

If humiliation is part of the job description, then let's stop calling it entertainment and start calling it what it is: a system designed to chew women up like the Hunger Games. The format doesn't just allow this - it relies on it. Producers may hide behind "authenticity," but the truth is, they know exactly what they're doing. They don't cast women to tell their stories; they cast them to fit a pre-arranged narrative. One that keeps viewers outraged, invested, and ready to tear someone apart by episode three.

So no, women shouldn't *expect* this. But as long as this is the blueprint, it's exactly what they'll get.

# CHAPTER 7:
# THE PSYCHOLOGY OF TROLLS

## STEPFORD CALLED - THEY WANT THEIR GENDER ROLES BACK

It's not just that women are trolled. It's *how* they're trolled. The abuse isn't generic - it's gendered, targeted, and often violent. While both men and women are harassed online, research shows that women are more likely to be threatened with sexual violence, stalked across platforms, and subjected to character assassinations that focus on their appearance, sexuality, or perceived "attitude". It's as though the internet decided it wanted 1952 back and went full Stepford.

One study found that nearly 60% of women and girls have faced some form of online violence. What's more, the abuse ramps up in frequency and severity when the woman in question is opinionated, visible, or - God forbid - funny. The data tracks: women in public roles are routinely warned to "shut up or else," with the "else" including rape threats, doxing, and coordinated pile-ons.

And the cherry on top? Algorithms love this stuff. Misogynistic content tends to get engagement, and engagement gets boosted.

## THE ALGORITHM HAS NO CONSCIENCE

It's easy to believe that the hate is personal. That the pile-on happened because of *me* - my face, my voice, my refusal to play the docile wife. But when I zoomed out, something became chillingly clear: it wasn't personal. It was algorithmic.

Social media platforms aren't neutral arenas - they're machines engineered to reward engagement, and nothing gets people frothing at the mouth quite like a woman who isn't easy to digest. The more controversial I was made to look, the more clicks, comments, and shares it generated. The algorithm doesn't care *why* people are angry - it just notices that they are and gives them more of what keeps their thumbs moving. It doesn't have a conscience, it has a KPI.

Researchers from University College London and the University of Kent released a study in 2024 showing that platforms like TikTok quadrupled the amount of misogynistic content shown to users in just five days. It was like training a dog with rage pellets. Anger, blame, and anti-women narratives weren't just allowed - they were *promoted.* That isn't an accident. That's the business model.

It wasn't just TikTok. Dublin City University's Anti-Bullying Centre found the same patterns on YouTube Shorts - algorithms fast-tracking viewers straight into what's now being called the "manosphere", a digital boys' club where women are either worshipped, blamed, or destroyed.

So, no - the hate wasn't *about* me. It was about what I represented. A woman who didn't fawn, a woman who dared to have standards. In a digital landscape built on outrage, my refusal to conform to expectations was prime content. I wasn't trending because people hated me, I was trending because the algorithm knew they *would.*

The irony? These very same people were being radicalised one swipe at a time, while accusing *me* of being the dangerous one.

## CSI: COMMENT SECTION

Truthfully, I don't even fully blame the viewers. The edit meant that they didn't see the real story. They saw what they were meant to see: a perfectly sliced, villain-scripted version of me and a harmless, gormless edit of him. It was expert manipulation.

We spent hours - forensic hours - trying to figure out what was wrong with these people. My friends and I became, war room strategists swapping theories, comparing screenshots, mapping a cult.

Yes, it was cultish. The way they latched onto a version of reality that didn't exist. The way they clung to it, violently, as if letting go would unravel their own identities. You could present them with facts, footage, the missing context, and they'd still choose hate. They *needed* a villain. And unfortunately for them, I could cut my eyes on cue.

## THE DIGITAL PLAYGROUND FOR DISORDERED PERSONALITIES

Social media has evolved into an ecosystem that inadvertently nurtures certain maladaptive personality traits, particularly those associated with Cluster B disorders. The design of these platforms - driven by algorithms that reward intensity over accuracy, performance over authenticity -

creates ideal conditions for traits like narcissism, emotional manipulation, and impulsivity to not only survive, but thrive. What might be disordered behaviour in real life becomes validated, even celebrated, in the digital space.

## THE ALGORITHM LOVES A NARCISSIST

It turns out the people glued to their phones shouting into the void for likes and followers might not just be attention-hungry - they might be diagnosable. Studies show a strong link between excessive social media use and traits tied to narcissistic personality disorder (NPD). One study even found that men who frequently post selfies often score higher in narcissism and psychopathy-textbook "Dark Triad" stuff.

It gets better: another study on undergraduates found that heavy emoji use among men was tied to Machiavellianism and neuroticism. In short, the more emojis, the greater the manipulation. Among women, overuse of emojis showed a link to narcissism. Cute on the surface, chaotic underneath.

Social media thrives on performance. It rewards the loudest, the neediest, the most curated versions of ourselves. So, it's no surprise that people with narcissistic tendencies gravitate to platforms that let them collect validation like digital trophies.

Speaking of Narcissists, I just finished the last season of *You*. Joe Goldberg? Narcissist. Psychopath. Literary fuckboy with a saviour complex. Critics hated the ending, but to me it nailed a narcissistic collapse - not guilt, just the horror of losing control of the narrative. They called it the season finale - but is he down and out for good? Doubt it.

## BORDERLINE, ONLINE

People with borderline personality disorder (BPD) aren't immune to the pull either. A study in *Frontiers in Psychiatry* found that individuals with BPD are more prone to social media addiction, drawn to the rush of instant feedback and the illusion of constant connection.

The emotional instability and abandonment anxiety that often come with BPD make social media a double-edged sword - both a temporary fix and a long-term trigger. The highs are high, the crashes are brutal, and the platform keeps the cycle spinning.

## WHAT THIS MEANS FOR ALL OF US

The intersection of social media and personality disorders isn't a footnote - it's the headline. It's reshaping how we argue, perform, and exist online. Algorithms reward extremes. The more unhinged, inflammatory, or emotionally volatile the content, the faster it spreads. Which means the loudest, most disordered behaviour gets the biggest spotlight.

We've built a digital culture that glorifies chaos, punishes nuance, and turns harassment into a spectator sport.

If we don't start recognising how mental health intersects with online behaviour, we'll keep mistaking dysfunction for influence - and calling it engagement. What we really need isn't just digital literacy. It's emotional literacy. Because right now, outrage is the currency - and we're all paying the price.

## HURRICANE MILTON WAS EASIER TO REASON WITH

Meanwhile, I'm being called unhinged by people who spend their evenings writing manifestos in the comments section of a Network 4 Instagram page. The irony is so thick it's practically edible.

Janey messaged me in shock: "You're trending above Hurricane Milton!!" We both burst out laughing. The only thing more chaotic than a tropical storm is a mob with WiFi and no critical thinking.

We used to think they were watching us, but in the end, we were watching them - unravel, perform, project. It was theatre. Ugly, badly written theatre. But theatre all the same.

Even when the cracks started to show, even when it was becoming obvious that Orton wasn't the perfect gentleman they'd been sold, the viewers doubled down. I was still called toxic, and he was still protected like he was a national treasure. Because once people have decided who the villain is, they can't let go of it. They'd rather rewrite reality than admit they might have been wrong.

## WOMEN POLICING WOMEN: A NATIONAL SPORT

The worrying part wasn't the men calling me names - it was the women. The ones who seemed to hate me with a kind of fever. Who watched a show where I was lied to, humiliated, and edited into a caricature... and still decided *I* was the problem?

It's easy to dismiss them as bored or bitter, but there's something deeper going on. A kind of cultural conditioning. A lifelong subscription to internalised misogyny. Because society teaches women that there's only so much space. Only so much likeability. Only so much room at the table. So, when a woman steps out of line - when she's too loud, too sexual, too angry, too unbothered - we are sometimes the first to come for her. Not because we're bad people, but because we've been trained to believe it's our job.

Women are led to believe that because there's only so much room "at the top" for women, that we need to fight for it, so if someone "at the top" isn't behaving as expected, they need to be punished, brought down, and the space made for those people who see themselves as "more worthy". Instead of making more space for a greater range of women, women are made to fight amongst themselves for a seat at the table.

They'll say things like, "She should have behaved better," or "Well, she did come across badly." As if that excuses the hate. As if the punishment fits the edit they're given.

Psychologists have a name for this: **internalised sexism**. It's the invisible wiring that makes women defend men they don't know while tearing down women they don't like. And it's no accident. It's by design. Because a woman standing up for herself is threatening. But a woman joining in the pile-on? That's safe. That's familiar. That's normalised.

And so, they came - not with questions, but with certainty. Not to understand, but to condemn.

## WHEN MISOGYNY COMES WITH A MANICURE

It was predictable – the women. Women who should've known better. Women who saw another woman on TV and wanted to destroy her. At first, I found it surprising. But the deeper I looked, the clearer it became: a lot of this wasn't just misogyny, it was *internalised misogyny.*

Internalised sexism is when women absorb the very ideas that oppress them - like a virus that turns the host against itself. It's what makes some women instinctively defend a man they've never met, while foaming at the mouth over a woman they've got to know over two episodes. It's what convinces them that any woman who dares to speak out, stand up, or deviate from "nice" must be arrogant, manipulative, or worse - a threat.

There's also the idea that male validation means more than women's approval, therefore women will throw other women under the bus to climb over them to be the ones soaking up male approval. The ultimate Pick Me energy.

"She's wrong and not worthy so like me instead because I'm not like that."

Social media is the perfect arena for this kind of behaviour. It gives people an audience, a dopamine hit, and most importantly - an outlet. When reality TV paints a woman as "abusive," internalised sexism does the rest. Women become judge, jury, and digital executioner, because when you've been conditioned to compete with other women for approval, the easiest target is always the one society has already marked as too loud, too confident, or simply too much.

## WHEN TRUTH DOESN'T MATTER

At some point, it became clear that even if the viewers knew the truth, the raw, unfiltered truth of my experience, they wouldn't care. Not really. They'd already decided who I was. By that point they hated me so much they'd say I deserved it.

I stopped hoping the truth would save me. I stopped hoping that once viewers realised what had actually happened - the manipulation, the secrets, the lies, the editing - they'd come around. That they'd say, *"Oh, maybe we got this wrong."* But deep down, I knew they wouldn't. Especially not the women. Because by then, it wasn't about what was *true,* it was about what they *felt.* And what they felt was that I deserved it.

The storyline had become emotional currency. I was cast as the villain, and they'd invested in that version of me. They were angry on his behalf, like they'd birthed him themselves and savage toward a woman who wouldn't just shut up and behave. Once people are emotionally invested in their hate, the truth becomes inconvenient. Compassion becomes optional. Facts are just noise.

Even if I'd held up evidence on national TV, I believe many of them still would have found a reason to hate me. Because the hate wasn't about me - it was about what I represented. I was a woman who didn't perform softness. I was a woman who said, "No, I don't like him," and meant it. I was a woman who didn't apologise for making people feel uncomfortable.

When the narrative is *how dare she not like him* - no amount of truth stands a chance.

So, I kept my mouth shut. Not out of fear but out of pure exhaustion. What was the point? You can't reason with people who aren't interested in reason. You can't offer honesty to an audience that only wants a performance.

They stop being open to nuance. They stop being curious. And worst of all, they stop being human about it.

## FALSE CONSENSUS: THE ECHO CHAMBER IN YOUR HEAD

There's actually a psychological explanation for it - not that it makes it any less twisted. It's one of the most damaging psychological traps in this whole circus is something called the *false consensus effect.* This is when people believe that their opinions are far more widely shared than they really are. On social media, this effect becomes turbocharged because if you see five comments that agree with you, your brain convinces you *everyone* must agree. And if everyone agrees, it *must* be true, right?

That's how hate spreads with such velocity. It's not just that someone dislikes you - it's that they believe *everyone* does. That you're a collective enemy. Suddenly, it's not one opinion among many; it's "the truth," validated by emojis and comment likes. From there, people feel emboldened - even righteous - in their abuse. It's no longer seen as bullying; it's seen as justice.

This effect is particularly brutal in reality TV because the edit hands viewers a neatly packaged version of you - simplified, exaggerated, emotionally engineered. And once people decide who you are based on that version, the false consensus takes over. They see other people saying the same things - "she's cold", "she's toxic,", "she emasculated him" - and they start to believe it's not an opinion but a fact. A fact they are now duty-bound to enforce in your DMs.

Here's the real kicker: when someone *doesn't* agree with the mob, they're usually too scared to say so. Therefore, the silence of dissenters just fuels the illusion that there's a consensus. It's a vacuum - one that amplifies hate and silences nuance. In that kind of environment, there's no space for truth. There's just the narrative. And you? You become whatever they need you to be.

## EMASCULATION BY EDIT

Some of the most emotional abuse I received came from men - men who weren't even on the show. I used to wonder: *Why are you so angry? What part of this has anything to do with you?*

Then it hit me that for some men, watching a woman on national TV hold a man to account, challenge him, or simply say, "No thanks" is a form of emasculation. It's not logical - it's emotional. It threatens a deeply embedded narrative about what men are owed: respect, submission, a second chance, silence. When a woman deviates from that script - when she rejects the match, raises her voice, or refuses to stroke a man's ego on command - it hits them where it hurts: their entitlement.

In that moment, they're not just watching a show, they're projecting. Onto me. Onto him. Onto every woman who's ever told them, *"You're not it"*. It becomes personal, even if it isn't.

## BICEPS, BRAVADO, AND A SHAKY SENSE OF SELF

Psychologically, this ties into *precarious manhood theory* - the idea that masculinity isn't a fixed state, but a fragile status that must be constantly earned and defended. So, when a woman dares to be visible, confident, or simply uninterested - especially in public - it can be perceived as an attack. That perceived threat doesn't lead to reflection; it leads to retaliation. Shame turns to rage, and instead of sitting with their discomfort, some men hurl it back at the woman who made the mistake of existing unapologetically.

It drives them to your page. Not to understand. Not to discuss. But to reclaim dominance - through insults, threats, and digital chest-beating. Because if they can tear you down, even anonymously, they get to feel powerful again.

In some cases, the messages read like breakup texts from men I'd never dated. Wounded. Emotional. Seething with this theatrical sense of betrayal -I'd stomped on their masculinity just by not fawning over a man on camera.

It was unhinged. Men telling me I was everything wrong with women, that I was cold, heartless, and arrogant. They told me that I'd never find love and I deserved to be alone. As if my onscreen persona had somehow reached into their childhood trauma and pressed every button.

That's when I realised - this wasn't about me. This was about them. It was about what I represented. I was a woman who didn't perform submission. A woman who didn't need male approval to feel valid. For some men, this was a direct threat to their entire worldview.

When masculinity feels under threat, some men respond not with introspection, but with aggression. That sense of inadequacy quickly curdles into a need to dominate - to put women "back in their place." Often, it doesn't look like shouting or fists. It looks like subtle emotional abuse, passive-aggressive sabotage, and online cruelty disguised as commentary.

This isn't just personal insecurity - it's cultural. We live in a world that rewards men for punishing women who won't shrink. So, when a woman dares to be visible, or uninterested, some men don't just take it badly - they take it personally. And now, they don't need a mob, they just need Wi-Fi.

## WHEN THE COMMENTS SECTION NEEDS THERAPY

In the end, the trolls weren't just reacting to a TV show - they were reacting to their own unresolved wounds, warped beliefs, and algorithm-fed rage. It was never really about me. I was just the placeholder for whatever woman had once bruised their ego, challenged their authority, or simply dared to exist without apology.

Between internalised misogyny, the dopamine loops of digital outrage, and algorithms that serve up hate like it's a lunchtime meal deal, social media has become the perfect breeding ground for dysfunction disguised as entertainment. They weren't watching to understand. They were watching to punish.

And maybe that's the saddest part: that we've created a culture where a woman saying "no", or just being herself, is enough to mobilise a mob with direct access to my DMs.

And this chapter? It's not about revenge. It's a post-mortem - on what happens when reality TV stops being a show and starts being a mirror, reflecting back all the ugliest parts of us.

## THE REAL VILLAIN WEARS A RATINGS BADGE

In the end, the trolls and the show were just symptoms of a bigger issue. The real villain wasn't a badly edited TV character or an anonymous commenter - it was a culture that loves to watch women burn at the stake and calls it entertainment. The show must know this, because it's their formula - season after season, it's always the women bearing the brunt of the hate. And as long as that's the narrative, the only way forward is to rewrite the script entirely. This is a long tradition of watching women be hunted, persecuted, punished, for mass entertainment. A 21st century - witch hunt.

But one has to recognise that the show's purpose is to make money, and if they know that this formula wins them high ratings, then who is really to blame here? If viewers crave this narrative and the show delivers, isn't it a reflection of a society that needs to change as much as the show itself? As long as that's the narrative, the only way forward is to rewrite the script entirely, because until then, we are all just feeding the beast that thrives on tearing women down. In the end, the only way to break the cycle is to shine a light on the machinery behind the scenes. By dragging the truth into the light and refusing to play nice, we can force reality TV to be less exploitative - and maybe, one day, even human.

# CHAPTER 8:

# THE WELFARE ILLUSION: LEGALLY COVERED, MORALLY BANKRUPT

Before filming began, we were told there were measures in place to protect us. "Welfare team,", "psych support", "duty of care" - phrases dropped into conversation like warm safety nets. It all sounded very official. Very comforting. And very misleading.

In reality, the so-called welfare measures felt more like PR gestures than meaningful systems. The 'support' existed, technically. There were phone numbers, vague check-ins, the occasional therapy session dangled like a carrot. But when it actually mattered - when real concerns were raised, when lines were crossed, when things felt unsafe - suddenly, that safety net vanished. Or worse, tightened around your neck.

I wasn't naive. I didn't expect luxury, or even fairness. But I did expect the basics -standard safeguarding, a genuine interest in our welfare, and some sense that if I raised a concern about my match, it would actually be taken seriously. Instead, I was met with rehearsed responses and subtle deflection -the kind designed to make you question your own perception. And while I could see through it, I know how damaging that kind of gaslit doubt can be for younger cast members still learning to trust their instincts.

The welfare team often felt like a separate arm of production. Less there to care, and more there to monitor, manage, and mollify. You weren't supported; you were contained. Kept just happy enough to keep filming. Just calm enough to stay on set. If you weren't then you were the problem. It wasn't the trauma, the man, nor the circumstances. It was *You.*

There's a reason participants are reluctant to speak up until after the show airs. And then after - well after - they're carefully directed to *the tabloid press* to tell their story where they're manipulated into divulging their truth to a paper that doesn't honour it but sensationalises it, crafting whatever version the show needs to continue to push its chosen narrative. Your truth gets distorted long before it hits print - through senior welfare staff vague assurances and emotional minimising, tabloid fodder, and the endless churn of social media discourse.

Based on what I later learned, I quickly realised that 'duty of care' doesn't mean what you think it means. It doesn't mean they'll protect you from harm. It means they'll protect themselves *from liability*. There's a difference. A massive one. That was the moment I realised I wasn't in safe hands. I was in *jazz* hands - hands that cared about optics, about footage, about staying on the right side of legal - but did not care about *me*.

That's the fallacy. The illusion. The lie wrapped in legalese. They tell you there's a welfare team, but no one's coming to save you. You are cast, contracted, and commodified. Once you stop performing the way they want; the duty of care becomes damage control. They'll tell the public they supported you. They'll say you had access to therapy, and that a welfare officer was always available. But in truth, the access doesn't mean action. Being told you can call someone isn't the same as being *heard*. Being watched isn't the same as being *seen*. And being offered care in theory is not care at all.

It's the young ones I feel sorry for. The average reality TV contestant in the UK is in their twenties - young, hopeful, and often still figuring out who they are. They go on these shows chasing opportunity, visibility, a shot at their dream. But dreams sold in edit suites and production rooms come with a cost they can't always see until it's too late. The emotional fallout, the online abuse, the misrepresentation - these things don't just blow over. They follow you into jobs, relationships, and mental health battles long after the credits roll.

I'm nearly 50. I know what's what. I've got enough life experience to recognise when I'm being handled, manipulated, used. But these young people don't. Not yet. And by the time they figure it out, the damage is often done- broadcast and online forever.

That's what they don't show - how easily your instincts can be dismantled when control is disguised as care. This book is a warning. For the younger women who haven't learned yet to trust their gut over a script.

In the end, I realised the real duty of care was mine - to myself. I had to leave with whatever scraps of sanity I had left. To speak when I could. To survive the story, they tried to tell about me, because their priority was never my welfare. Their priority was the storyline.

And they got it. At my expense.

They'll say something different, no doubt. They always do. But in my view - based on my experience and what the regulations require - they failed me. They failed to protect my safety. I was matched with someone who had an STD they knew about, and they didn't tell me. That wasn't just a breach of trust, it was a violation of my right to make an informed decision about my own body.

They denied me informed consent. I was expected to enter a process without knowing something that should have been non-negotiable. From my experience it felt like they failed to carry out any meaningful risk assessment. If they had, they would have seen the danger in that match. Either they didn't do it, or they did and ignored what it told them. Either way, they decided it was worth the risk because it made good TV.

I was deliberately misrepresented. I understand how reality TV works, but what they did wasn't just editing, it was construction. They created a version of me that was easier to hate. More provocative. More clickable.

The rules are pretty clear. If you're putting ordinary people into extraordinary situations - strangers, pressure, cameras, the internet - then you have a responsibility to look after them. That means checking for risks, being honest about what could happen, making sure people understand what they're walking into, and offering support when it all starts to unravel. It's not complicated. It's supposed to be about care, dignity, and doing the right thing when no one's watching.

When I look back now, the part that still shocks me isn't just what happened, it's how easily it was allowed to happen. There are rules. There are guidelines. They're supposed to protect people like me, people stepping into something unfamiliar and trusting the process to be safe. But what I experienced wasn't care. It was calculation. Every safeguard that was meant to be there - honesty, consent, aftercare – was a fallacy.

To top it off, this all-powerful "duty of care" team - who had no issue ignoring actual welfare concerns, got spooked by a few Instagram posts and a Ms Dynamite verse. Suddenly I was a security risk. They threatened to call the police. Over lyrics. Not when I was questioning their ethics. Not when I was matched with someone they hadn't vetted properly. But when I posted a rap.

That's the reality behind reality TV: the duty of care is only as strong as the people willing to uphold it - and if it wasn't so serious, the whole concept here would be farcical.

They weren't afraid of negligence. They weren't afraid of reputational damage. They were afraid of exposure - of being named. That's what rattled them. Not the harm they allowed, but the possibility that someone might say it out loud.

It's all smoke and mirrors- and your welfare is just part of the illusion.[1]

1 Disclaimer: The events and experiences described in this chapter reflect the author's personal recollection and perspective. Some dialogue has been paraphrased, condensed, or altered for clarity. Names and identifying details have been changed or withheld to protect privacy. Interpretations of motives and behaviour are the author's own and based on how they were experienced at the time. References to medical information, emotional impact, or duty of care reflect the author's personal understanding and are not intended as legal claims or factual statements about any individual or organisation.

# CHAPTER 9:
# PEACE, POWER, AND THE LAST WORD

## FROM SWEET VALLEY TO SAVAGE REALITY

Some of my followers know that growing up, I used to love reading - Sweet Valley High, Just William, you name it, I was devouring books from a young age. (Fielder's bookstore, Wimbledon anyone?)

Picture me at ten years old, with my thick NHS glasses, lost in the pages of a good story. As life catches up, you lose the time, the focus, and the inclination to sit down and enjoy reading. That's why, for me, the fact that I've captured my experience in a book - and managed to publish it - makes it all feel worth it. If I get sued - I'll just add that to the sequel.

## THE REAL EXPERT WAS ME ALL ALONG

As I bring this story to a close, I can't help but reflect on the illusions that led me here. I stepped into the process with a genuine desire for personal growth, trusting that these so-called experts were truly qualified to help me understand myself better. I wanted to grow, to evolve - and to stop repeating the same patterns in relationships, expecting different results.

I've spent the last seven months trying to find a reason I could say *this, this* is why I was meant to do it- *this* is what the universe wanted. I was desperate to find meaning - something deeper that would stop me from drowning in regret. And this book... this is it. This is the reason. Through it, I've managed to pull purpose from the chaos. I've learned about the industry, about people, and why I avoid them, but most of all I've learned about myself.

## UNDOING QUIET DAMAGE

Through this journey, I can now see flaws in my own logic and patterns that I couldn't see before. While the show didn't give me the personal growth I was after, it did do me the favour of emotionally drop-kicking me into therapy.

I'd always thought therapy was just something Americans did between yoga and brunch. It felt indulgent. Dramatic. Definitely not for me. But at 49, I finally gave it a go. Turns out, acknowledging your trauma doesn't make you a victim. It makes you human.

Therapy made it clear I'd spent years doubting my own judgement because others refused to take accountability. My anger wasn't the problem - their denial was. Now, I push back. Hard.

I see things less foggy now, no longer shaped by the chaos I've lived through, but by the way I've clawed my way out of it - slightly feral but thriving.

## INTEGRITY OVER EGO

I was right all along, of course. When accountability is absent in relationships, it doesn't just cause pain, it distorts reality. It leaves the other person questioning themselves, carrying blame that was never theirs to hold. That's why I teach my daughter every day: perfection isn't the goal, integrity is. Owning your part - even when it's hard - is how you protect the people you care about.

I tell her never feel too proud to say the word *sorry*. Accountability doesn't make you weak - it makes you trustworthy. So many people now avoid it altogether, as if saying sorry costs more than staying silent, but it doesn't. The real cost is what it does to relationships when no one takes responsibility.

Some people treat "sorry" like it's a swear word - but you better learn to say it before you start burning bridges you need to cross later.

## MY DAUGHTER WILL KNOW, AND SO WILL HER DAUGHTERS

I can't control how others move through the world, but I can control what I pass on. The cycle stops with me. If I want her to know better, I have to show better - not just in words, but in how I rebuild, how I respond, how I rise.

My daughter is already strong. I just want to make sure the world doesn't convince her to doubt it.

This is how I rewrite the narrative on my terms. It's my chance to show my daughter, my grandchildren, and generations to come that even when others try to define you, you can always take back your story and turn a painful experience into something lasting, I can hold, that's mine.

## THE QUEEN AMINA EFFECT

My mum named me after Queen Amina of Zaria (present-day Nigeria), then spent my entire childhood shocked that she'd birthed someone so combative. But really - what did she expect? You name a girl after a warrior queen and act surprised when she starts swinging? Let that be a cautionary tale for anyone out there getting creative with baby names.

Queen Amina of Zaria - a 16th century - Hausa warrior who led armies, expanded empires, and, according to legend, had a deadly sexual appetite. My mum used to tell me from young, proudly, that Queen Amina would sleep with her captors and have them killed by morning. "She was a *notorious* warrior," she'd say laughing. I was four. What exactly I was meant to do with that information at that age, I don't know - but here we are.

She spent my childhood baffled that she'd raised someone so militant, but really - you name a girl after a warrior queen with a kill count and then act surprised when she won't back down in an argument?

## MASCULINE ENERGY, FEMININE CHAOS

Being casually told by a doctor, aged about ten, that I had high testosterone for a girl.

Add to that a few skewed family dynamics and personal experiences, and it's no surprise my view of masculinity ended up a bit distorted.

That's probably why I clung to the idea of a "masculine man" - for protection. Masculinity meant safety. Physical safety. But protection isn't just physical - it's emotional too. And that's where things usually fell short. Because protection without emotional safety? Isn't protection at all.

Masculine energy or not, I am -and always have been - a woman. A full-force, high-functioning, deeply feminine woman. And I wouldn't trade that ever. I love being a woman. And let's face it - if you think I'm a handful as a woman, imagine the chaos I'd unleash as a man. Now *that* would be something.

Loving being a woman doesn't mean it's a breeze - it means I've mastered the art of showing up anyway, eyelashes hanging, mood swinging, and still somehow holding it all together like a high functioning hot mess.

## SELF-LOVE ISN'T A SIDE HUSTLE

Let me say this loud enough for the women in the back: loving yourself -and saying it out loud - isn't vanity. It's self-worth. In my twenties, I kept hearing, "You think you're too nice," always from men I'd rejected. Which, translation: *"How dare you not find me irresistible?"* For a while, I wasted time trying to soften the blow - twisting myself into emotional origami so they wouldn't feel bruised by the word *no*. Then one day, I stopped performing. Now I just say, "Yes. Yes, I do." And I smile while I mean it.

We're living in an age where even female friendships can morph into competitive sport, and dating feels like emotional roulette. It's hard to hold onto your self-worth when everyone's projecting their insecurities like it's a group art project. But here's the truth: no one gets to define you unless you hand them the pen. So, keep your pen. Guard it like a family heirloom. Write your story like it's already a bestseller and make sure self-love is the main character.

## DIFFICULT WOMEN GET THINGS DONE

If I've learned anything, it's that you must advocate for yourself – loudly and unapologetically. No one's handing out gold stars for quiet resilience. Women are trained to be accommodating, to shrink themselves, to wait until it's "the right time." But the right time rarely announces itself - you've got to declare it. Stand up. Speak out. Send the email, say the thing, take up the space. Being your own advocate isn't aggressive - it's necessary. And honestly, if people find that intimidating, they can feel free to look away.

What's even shadier is when they try to flip it by using your *delivery* as the problem, not the point you're making. That's not feedback. That's gaslighting in a nicer font. It's a tactic - minimise the message by making the messenger sound "too much," "too direct," or "not nice enough." It's easier to dismiss a woman as aggressive than admit she's right.

Tone-policing isn't feedback - it's just people saying, "I'd agree with you if you said it in a gentler voice... and preferably not to me".

## PERIMENOPAUSAL WITH ADHD - AND SOMEHOW STILL RUNNING SHIT

For most of my life, I thought ADHD was a made-up excuse for bad behaviour - something kids were labelled with when parents couldn't be bothered to parent. That was the messaging. ADHD was for boys who threw chairs, not women who ran businesses.

But lately, I've started looking at my own patterns - half-finished projects, Olympic-level procrastination, hyper-focus on the most irrelevant details and the general sensation that my brain is a browser with 37 tabs open, four of which are playing music I can't find.

So, yeah. I'm coming around to the idea that maybe I have ADHD. Not a trauma response. Not an identity crisis. *Not a Cluster B diagnosis* - thank God. Just the good old-fashioned, garden variety executive dysfunction that makes you look high-functioning while your brain is busy trying to remember where you left your phone, which is in your hand.

So maybe I am neurologically spicy.

And as for perimenopause. Viewers really thought that was an insult. Like "perimenopausal bitch" was some kind of trump card. First: if I am, which I must be, congratulations. That makes me grown. Second: if you were a little closer to menopause, maybe you'd be less bothered. Try evolving. It's peaceful here.

## PEACE OVER PRODUCTION DRAMA

At this stage in my life, I'm chasing peace. I know, hilarious, considering I voluntarily entered the Hunger Games of reality TV. But that's the beauty of being a unique person - we contain contradictions. My mum used to say, "Feel the fear and do it anyway", and that mantra carried me straight out of my comfort zone and into a world I had no business entering. Do I have any regrets, given how it all unfolded? I used to. But then I wrote this, sharpened my voice, and gave my therapist a well-earned break. So, no - no regrets. Not now.

## THE SKINCARE SERMON YOU WERE WAITING FOR

And as for my skincare - because let's be honest, that's what you really came for, and I'm sorry I held out this long. Cleanse, tone, moisturise daily - morning and night. Pick products that actually suit your skin (not just what's trending), get a microdermabrasion now and then, slap on SPF like your life depends on it, splash your eyeballs a few times a day to keep the whites white, and for the love of everything holy: wash off your makeup. I don't care how tired you are - and drink some damn water. Hydrated skin doesn't just happen by accident.

## PEACE OVER PENIS™

Ultimately, I think having good skin at my age comes down to one thing: knowing when to extract yourself - gracefully or otherwise - from stressful and toxic situations and people who add zero value to your life. Stress is ageing. Full stop. Choose peace. Always. Over penis. Every time.

## THANKS, AND YOU'RE WELCOME

To every woman reading this: glow so bright they think it's good lighting. Thanks for calling me out when I *apparently* needed it - even though I was doing just fine, but sure. Consider the favour returned.

You held the mirror. I didn't flinch but growth happened.

Here's to peace that can't be disturbed, power that doesn't beg for permission, and progress that doesn't ask for applause. Thank you for reading my book - and for bullying me into baring my soul to strangers. It's been unexpectedly therapeutic, occasionally unhinged, and actually... kind of fun.

The End

# REFERENCES

## PRIMARY REFERENCES

Bearman, S. et al. (2024). *Internalised Misogyny: The Patriarchy Inside Our Heads.* Study on how internalised sexism leads women to adopt patriarchal behaviours toward themselves and others.

Einhorn, S. (2021). *From a Woman's Point of View: How Internalised Misogyny Affects Relationships Between Women.* Explores the complexities of female rivalry shaped by internalised misogyny.

McMullin, M. K. (2011). *Are Women Really Harder on Other Women? A Survey of Female Undergraduates' Perceptions of Intrasexual Competition.* Investigates how female competition and negative perceptions manifest among young women.

Include Consulting. *Unravelling the Dynamics of Women's Workplace Rivalry.* Article exploring microaggressions and undermining behaviours among women at work.

*The Feminist Times* (2022, May 16). *Are Women Trolled More on Social Media?* Coverage on gendered harassment online.

University College London & University of Kent (2024). Study on algorithmic amplification of misogynistic content on TikTok.

Dublin City University Anti-Bullying Centre (2024). Research into TikTok and YouTube Shorts promoting misogynistic and male supremacist content.

Skeggs, B. (Various). *DCU Research Summary.* Sociological analysis of gender, class, and reality television.

*Personality and Individual Differences Journal.* Study on selfie-posting and narcissism in men.

*Time Magazine.* Coverage on digital identity and narcissism trends.

*Frontiers in Psychiatry* (2024). Study on social media addiction in individuals with Borderline Personality Disorder (BPD).

*The Times UK* (2024). Analysis of emoji use and its connection to narcissistic and Machiavellian traits.

## CITED SOURCES


Pew Research Center (2020). *The Decline of Marriage and Rise of New Families.* https://www.pewresearch.org

U.S. Bureau of Labor Statistics & OECD Gender Data. Reports on rising education and workforce participation among Millennial and Gen Z women.

Institute for Family Studies (2021). *Attitudes Toward Gender Roles and Relationship Expectations Across Generations.* https://ifstudies.org

*Psychology of Women Quarterly* (2019). Research on psychological autonomy and self-efficacy in intimate relationships across generations.

Twenge, J. (n.d.). *iGen* and *Generation Me.* Research on generational psychology, gender dynamics, and independence. https://www.jeantwenge.com

https://en.wikipedia.org/wiki/Deep_Fake_Love?utm_source=chatgpt.com

https://www.theguardian.com/tv-and-radio/article/2024/may/07/the-circle-max-ai-netflix?utm_source=chatgpt.com

Printed in Great Britain
by Amazon

63303751R00057